ALLEN PARK PUBLIC LIBRARY #4
8100 Allen Road
Allen Park, MI 48101-1708
313-381-2425

D0982445

TEEN 302.3 B

At Issue

Are Social Networking
Sites Harmful?

Other Books in the At Issue Series:

At Issue

Are Social Networking Sites Harmful?

Noah Berlatsky, Book Editor

GREENHAVEN PRESS
A part of Gale, Cengage Learning

GALE
CENGAGE Learning®

Farmington Hills, Mich • San Francisco • New York • Waterville, Maine
Meriden, Conn • Mason, Ohio • Chicago

Elizabeth Des Chenes, *Director, Content Strategy*
Douglas Dentino, *Manager, New Product*

© 2015 Greenhaven Press, a part of Gale, Cengage Learning.

WCN: 01-100-101

Gale and Greenhaven Press are registered trademarks used herein under license.

For more information, contact:
Greenhaven Press
27500 Drake Rd.
Farmington Hills, MI 48331-3535
Or you can visit our Internet site at gale.cengage.com

ALL RIGHTS RESERVED.
No part of this work covered by the copyright herein may be reproduced, transmitted, stored, or used in any form or by any means graphic, electronic, or mechanical, including but not limited to photocopying, recording, scanning, digitizing, taping, Web distribution, information networks, or information storage and retrieval systems, except as permitted under Section 107 or 108 of the 1976 United States Copyright Act, without the prior written permission of the publisher.

For product information and technology assistance, contact us at

Gale Customer Support, 1-800-877-4253
For permission to use material from this text or product, submit all requests online at www.cengage.com/permissions

Further permissions questions can be e-mailed to permissionrequest@cengage.com

Articles in Greenhaven Press anthologies are often edited for length to meet page requirements. In addition, original titles of these works are changed to clearly present the main thesis and to explicitly indicate the author's opinion. Every effort is made to ensure that Greenhaven Press accurately reflects the original intent of the authors. Every effort has been made to trace the owners of copyrighted material.

Cover photograph reproduced by permission of Brand X Pictures.

LIBRARY OF CONGRESS CATALOGING-IN-PUBLICATION DATA

Are social networking sites harmful? / Noah Berlatsky, book editor.
    pages cm. -- (At issue)
    Includes bibliographical references and index.
    ISBN 978-0-7377-7151-0 (hardcover) -- ISBN 978-0-7377-7152-7 (pbk.)
    1. Online social networks. I. Berlatsky, Noah.
    HM742.A742 2015
    302.30285--dc23
                                                    2014019508

Printed in the United States of America
1 2 3 4 5 6 7 18 17 16 15 14

Contents

3 9082 12778 9702

ALLEN PARK PUBLIC LIBRARY #
8100 Allen Road
Allen Park, MI 48101-1708
313-381-2425

Introduction

Social media has transformed the way that people get news. In the past, if there was a danger of flooding in your neighborhood, you would hear about it from professional newscasts on television or the radio, or even from a newspaper.

For many people today, however, information about safety or emergency issues, such as a flood, would come through social media. Sometimes, people share reports from official sources. For example, when the Boston Police Department tweeted that they had captured a suspect in the bombing of the Boston Marathon in 2013, more than 140,000 people retweeted the notification, according to Dina Fine Maron in a June 7, 2013, *Scientific American* article. At other times, people may get information from friends and neighbors talking directly about their own experiences. For instance, when Hurricane Sandy struck the northeast in 2012, 25 percent of the conversation on Twitter about the event was devoted to individuals sharing images and video of the storm, according to Bruce Drake in an October 28, 2013, article at the Pew Research Center website.

Social media can help people get news more quickly, and social platforms can also provide information that might not otherwise be available—such as, in the case of Hurricane Sandy, whether friends and family are okay, which streets are impassable, and exactly what the damage looks like. Thus, on social media "each disaster sparks its own complex web of fast-paced information exchange,"[1] as Maron at *Scientific American* writes. Maron paraphrases Mark Keim, associate director for science in the Office of Environmental Health Emergencies at the US Centers for Disease Control and Prevention

---

1. Dina Fine Maron, "How Social Media Is Changing Disaster Response," *Scientific American*, June 7, 2013. http://www.scientificamerican.com/article/how-social-media-is-changing-disaster-response.

(CDC), who argues that social media "can both improve disaster response and allow affected populations to take control of their situation as well as feel empowered."[2]

However, there can be downsides and even dangers to the use of social media as a news source, especially during emergency situations. The most serious issue is inaccurate information. In recent incidents involving mass shootings, for example, social media users have followed police scanners and then posted what they heard on Twitter or other online platforms. These reports then made their way to professional media outlets, which broadcast them as fact.

Police talking on scanners are often speculating or trying to figure out what is happening themselves; they aren't necessarily a good source for accurate information. As a result, news sources that rely on them often get things wrong, sometimes in dangerous ways. Reports on the school shooting in Newtown, Connecticut, in 2012 misidentified the shooter as Ryan Lanza, when it was actually his brother Adam. Reports from the Boston Marathon bombing said that there were three bomb blasts, when actually there were only two. Errors like these could potentially endanger innocent people, yet they were perpetuated by official news sources eager to stay ahead of social media and beat their competitors with the latest breaking news. Television news reporter Dave Statter says, "We've gotten into a situation where the media's standard operating procedure has become report first, confirm second and correct third."[3]

Initial misinformation is bad enough. But social media can also make it difficult to correct errors. That is because mistakes on social media can have a wider reach than the subsequent attempts to correct those mistakes.

2. Ibid.
3. Quoted in Paul Farhi, "When News Breaks, Scanners and Social Media Can Create a Cloud of Errors for News Outlets," *Washington Post*, September 16, 2013. http://www.washingtonpost.com/lifestyle/style/news-outlets-often-stumble-in-quest-for-speed-and-accuracy/2013/09/16/e5444820-1f19-11e3-8459-657e0c72fec8_story.html.

Gilad Lotan, vice president of research and development for SocialFlow, a social networking software company, researched an incorrect tweet from 2011 that stated that during a protest in New York City, the NYC Police Department shut down airspace. Lotan found that the incorrect tweet was shared at its height at a rate of more than two hundred tweets every ten minutes. A correction that ran a half hour later was only shared at a peak rate of one hundred tweets per ten minutes. Four hours after the initial tweet, and three and a half hours after the correction, the initial erroneous tweet was still being shared more often than the correction.

Lotan noted that while incorrect information doesn't always beat out correct information, "People are much more likely to retweet what they want to be true, their aspirations and values."[4] Journalists and individuals could help minimize false information by taking more time to confirm stories, and by being sure to share and reshare any corrections. The dangers of misinformation from social media are not an inherent part of the technology, but rather are the result of people using the network in particular ways. With greater awareness of the hazards, people and news organizations can work to avoid them.

At Issue: Are Social Networking Sites Harmful? looks at these and other dangers and possibilities of social networking, including such issues as social media addiction, the relationship between social media and government repression, and online harassment of women and teens.

---

4. Gilad Lotan, "A Tale of Three Rumors," *Gilad Lotan Blog*, March 6, 2012. http://giladlotan.com/blog/page/2.

Social Media Data Collection Can Lead to Violations of Privacy

Andre Oboler, Kristopher Welsh, and Lito Cruz

Andre Oboler is chief executive officer of the Online Hate Prevention Institute and a postgraduate law student at Monash University. Kristopher Welsh is a lecturer in the School of Computing at the University of Kent. Lito Cruz is a teaching associate at Monash University and a part-time lecturer at Charles Sturt University. He holds a PhD in computer science from Monash University.

Social media data can be used to collect information about individuals by governments, businesses, journalists, employers, or social media platforms themselves. This data collection can result in numerous kinds of infringements of privacy. It could be used to manipulate voters, track activists, profile job applicants, or even reveal a user's physical movements. Social media platforms have given little consideration to the ethical issues raised. More needs to be done by both social media companies and users to prevent abuses of data.

Computational social science involves the collection, retention, use and disclosure of information to answer enquiries from the social sciences. As an instrument based discipline, the scope of investigation is largely controlled by the

Andre Oboler, Kristopher Welsh, and Lito Cruz, "The Danger of Big Data: Social Media as Computational Social Science," *First Monday*, vol.17, issue 7, July 2, 2012. Copyright © 2012 by Andre Oboler, Kristopher Welsh, and Lito Cruz. All rights reserved. Reproduced by permission.

parameters of the computer system involved. These parameters can include: the type of information people will make available, data retention policies, the ability to collect and link additional information to subjects in the study, and the processing ability of the system. The capacity to collect and analyze data sets on a vast scale provides leverage to reveal patterns of individual and group behaviour.

The Danger of Data

The revelation of these patterns can be a concern when they are made available to business and government. It is, however, precisely business and government who today control the vast quantities of data used for computational social science analysis.

> *The risk posed by the ubiquity of computational social science tools . . . poses serious questions about the impact that those who control the data and the tools can have on society as a whole.*

Some data should not be readily available: this is why we have laws restricting the use of wiretaps, and protecting medical records. The potential damage from inappropriate disclosure of information is sometimes obvious. However, the potential damage of multiple individually benign pieces of information being combined to infer, or a large dataset being analysed to reveal, sensitive information (or information which may later be considered sensitive) is much harder to foresee. A lack of transparency in the way data is analysed and aggregated, combined with a difficulty in predicting which pieces of information may later prove damaging, means that many individuals have little perception of potential adverse effects of the expansion in computational social science.

Both the analysis of general trends and the profiling of individuals can be investigated through social sciences. Applications of computational social science in the areas of social anthropology and political science can aid in the subversion of democracy. More than ever before, groups or individuals can be profiled, and the results used to better manipulate them. This may be as harmless as advertising for a particular product, or as damaging as political brainwashing. At the intersection of these examples, computational social science can be used to guide political advertising; people can be sold messages they will support and can be sheltered from messages with which they may disagree. Access to data may rest with the incumbent government, with those able to pay, or with those favoured by powerful data-rich companies.

Politics and Beyond

Under its new terms of service, Google could for instance significantly influence an election by predicting messages that would engage an individual voter (positively or negatively) and then filtering content to influence that user's vote. The predictions could be highly accurate making use of a user's e-mail in their Google provided Gmail account, their search history, their Google+ updates and social network connections, and their online purchasing history through Google Wallet, data in their photograph collection. The filtering of information could include "recommended" videos in YouTube; videos selectively chosen to highlight where one political party agrees with the user's views and where another disagrees with them. In Google News, articles could be given higher or lower visibility to help steer voters into making "the right choice".

Such manipulation may not be immediately obvious; a semblance of balance can be given with an equal number of positive and negative points made against each party. What computational social science adds is the ability to predict the effectiveness of different messages for different people. A message with no resonance for a particular voter may seem to objectively provide balance, while in reality making little impact.

Such services could not only be sold, but could be used by companies themselves to block the election of officials whose agenda runs contrary to their interests.

The ability to create such detailed profiles of individuals extends beyond the democratic process. The risk posed by the ubiquity of computational social science tools, combined with an ever-increasing corpus of data, and free of the ethical restrictions placed on researchers, poses serious questions about the impact that those who control the data and the tools can have on society as a whole. Traditionally, concerns about potential abuses of power focus on government and how its power can be limited to protect individuals; that focus needs to widen.

Social Media Data for Business

Social media systems contain particularly valuable information. This data derives its value from its detail, personal nature, and accuracy. The semi-public nature of the data means it is exposed to scrutiny within a user's network; this increases the likelihood of accuracy when compared to data from other sources. The social media data stores are owned and controlled by private companies. Applications such as Facebook, LinkedIn, and the Google suite of products (including Google search, YouTube, DoubleClick and others), are driven by information sharing, but monetized through internal analysis of the gathered data—a form of computational social science. The data is used by four classes of users: business clients, government, other users within the social media platform, and the platform provider itself.

Business clients draw on this computational social science when they seek to target their advertisements. Facebook, for example, allows advertisers to target users based on variables that range from standard demographics such as age, gender, and geographical location to more personal information such as sexual preferences. Users can also be targeted based on interests, associations, education level and employer. The Facebook platform makes this data (in aggregated form) available to advertisers for a specific purpose, yet Facebook's standard user interface can also be used as a general computational social science tool for other purposes.

The very existence of social media can . . . promote government's agenda.

To take an example, the Australian Bureau of Statistics (ABS) estimates the current population of Australia at 22.5 million. The Facebook advertising platform gives an Australia population (on Facebook) of 9.3 million; over 41 percent of the national population. As there is less coverage at the tails, Facebook has only 0.29 million people over 64, while the ABS says there are 3.06 million Australians over 65, the sample for some age ranges must be approaching the entire population and may provide a very good model as a computational social science tool. For example, research shows that about two percent of the Australia population is not heterosexual. From the Facebook advertising platform, we can readily [select] a population of Australians, aged 18 to 21, who are male, and whose sexual preference is for men. The platform immediately tells us the population size is 11,580 people. By comparing this to the total size of the Australian male Facebook population who expressed a sexual preference, we can see this accounts for 2.89 percent of this population, indicating that the data available to Facebook is of similar utility to that available to social scientists for research.

Data for Government

The second class of users of social media as computational social science tools is governmental. This is demonstrated by the U.S. government's demands to Twitter (via court orders) for data on Wikileaks founder Julian Assange and those connected to him. The court order was only revealed after Twitter took legal action to lift a court imposed censorship order relating to the requests. The Wikileaks affair demonstrates how government can act when it sees social media as acting against its interests.

The very existence of social media can also promote government's agenda. During the Iranian elections, for example, Twitter was asked not to take their service off-line for scheduled maintenance. In another example, the U.S. State Department provided training "using the Internet to effect social change" to Egyptian dissidents between 2008 and 2010, then sought (unsuccessfully) to keep social media access available during the January 2011 Egyptian anti-government protests. The Egyptian effort was defeated after Egypt responded by taking the entire country off the Internet, a move perhaps more in response to the U.S. than the protestors. While social media might enable activism, computational social science favours the state or at least those with power. Computational social science tools combined with social media data can be used to reconstruct the movements of activists, to locate dissidents, and to map their networks. Governments and their security services have a strong interest in this activity.

Social Media Data, Journalists, and Providers

The third class of actors are other social media platform users. Journalist Ada Calhoun has described as an epiphany that left her "freaked out" the realisation that anyone could research her just as she researched others while writing their obituaries. In her article, Calhoun reflected that some amateur experts on the anarchic message board 4chan, or professional experts working for government agencies, could likely find out far more than she could. The everyday danger that can result when anyone can research anyone else can be demonstrated through two scenarios:

Scenario one involves Mary who has been a Facebook user for some years. Through Facebook Mary reconnected with an old friend Fred. As time went on, Mary and Fred grew closer and became a couple. One day Mary logged into her Facebook account and noticed that Fred has still not updated his details to say he is in a relationship with her. This makes Mary feel very insecure, and causes her to begin doubting Fred's intentions. Due to this discovery, Mary broke off her relationship with Fred.

Joe applied to a company as a Human Resource team leader. The hiring manager, Bob, found Joe's resume appealing and considered him a good candidate. Bob decides to check Joe's Facebook information. On Joe's publically viewable wall, Bob sees several pictures of Joe in what Bob considers to be "questionable settings". The company never called Joe for an interview. Joe has been given no opportunity to explain, nor any explanation on why his application was rejected.

Computational science can help a company like Facebook correctly profile its users, showing the right advertisements to the right people so as to maximize revenue.

Both Mary and Bob used Facebook as a computational tool to extract selected information as part of an investigation into the social dynamics of society, or in these cases, a particular individual's interactions with society. In this sense, Facebook could be considered a computational social science tool. Mary's inference may be based on a wider realisation that Fred's interactions with her are all in private and not part of his wider representation of himself. Bob may have drawn his conclusions from a combination of text, pictures, and social interactions.

These situations are far from hypothetical. Research released in November 2011 by Telstra, Australia's largest telecommunications company, revealed that over a quarter of Australian bosses were screening job candidates based on social media. At the start of 2012 the Australia Federal Police began an advertising campaign designed to warn the public of the need to protect their reputation online. The advertisement featured a job interview where the interviewer consults a paper resume then proceeds to note various positive attributes about the candidate; all seems to be going very well. The interviewer then turns to his computer screen and adds "and I see from your recent online activity you enjoy planking from high rise buildings, binge drinking, and posting embarrassing photos of your friends online". The advertisement is an accurate picture of the current approach, which takes place at the level of one user examining another. Computational social science may soon lead to software programs that automatically complete pre-selection and filtering of candidates for employment.

The final class or actor we consider are social media platform providers themselves. While Facebook provides numerous metrics to profile users for advertisers, far more data and scope for analysis is available to a platform provider like Facebook itself. Internet advertisements are often sold on a "cost per-click" (CPC) or "cost per-impression" (CPM—with M indicating costs typically conveyed per-thousand impressions). Thus, Facebook may maximize advertising revenue by targeting advertisements to achieve the greatest possible number of clicks for a given number of impressions. This maximization of the click-through rate (CTR) can be achieved using a wealth of hidden information to model which users are most likely to respond to a particular advertisement. Computational science can help a company like Facebook correctly profile its users, showing the right advertisements to the right people so as to maximize revenue. But what else can a company like Facebook or Google do? This depends on the data they hold.

Triangulation, Breadth, and Depth

While horizontal expansion of computational social science allows greater access to selected aggregate data, vertical expansion allows larger operators to add depth to their models. This depth is a result of triangulation, a method originally from land surveying. Triangulation gives a confirmation benefit by using additional data points to increase the accuracy and confidence in a measurement. In a research context triangulation allows for information from multiple sources to be combined in a way that can expose underlying truths and increase the certainty of conclusions.

Social media platforms have added to their data either by acquiring other technology companies, as Google did when acquiring DoubleClick and YouTube, or by moving into new fields as Facebook did in when it created "Facebook Places": a foursquare-like geolocation service. From a computational social science perspective, geolocation services in particular add high value information. Maximising the value of information requires a primary key that connects this data with existing information; a Facebook user ID, or a Google account name provides just such a key.

The *breadth of an account* measures how many types of online interaction the one account connects. It lets the company providing the account know about a wider slice of a user's life. Three situations are possible. The first involves distinct accounts on multiple sites and allows no overlap of data: what occurs on one site stays on that site. The second situation is where there is a single traceable login, for example your e-mail address, which is used on multiple sites but where the sites are independent. Someone, or some computational social science tool, with access to the datasets could aggregate the data. The third possibility is a single login with complete data sharing between sites. All the data is immediately related and available to any query the underlying company devises. It is this last scenario that forms the Holy Grail for companies like Facebook and Google, and causes the most concern for users.

The announcement by Alma Whitten, Google's Director of Privacy, Product and Engineering in January 2012 that Google would aggregate its data and "treat you as a single user across all our products" has led to a sharp response from critics. Jeffrey Chester, executive director of the Center for Digital Democracy, told the *Washington Post*: "There is no way a user can comprehend the implication of Google collecting across platforms for information about your health, political opinions and financial concerns." In the same article, Common Sense Media chief executive James Steyer states bluntly that "Google's new privacy announcement is frustrating and a little frightening".

> *Accounts that are identity-verified, frequently updated, and used across multiple aspects of a person's life present the richest data and pose the greatest risk.*

The *depth of an account* measures the amount of data an account connects. There are three possible situations. The first is an anonymous login with no connection to personal details, the virtual profile is complete in and of itself—it may or may not truthfully represent the real world. The second situation is an account where user details are verified, for example a university login that is only provided once a student registers and identification papers have been checked. A number of online services and virtual communities are now using this model and checking government issued identification to verify age. The third situation involves an account that has a verified identity aggregated with other data collected from additional sources, for example, a credit card provider knows who its customers are, as well as where they have been and what they have bought. The temporal nature of the data is also a matter of depth; your current relationship status has less depth than your complete relationship history.

Facebook's Timeline feature signifies as large a change to depth as Google's policy change does to breadth. Timeline lets users quickly slide to a previous point in time, unearthing social interactions that had long been buried. A Facebook announcement on 24 January 2012 informed the world that Timeline was not optional and would in a matter of weeks be rolled out across all Facebook profiles.

As Sarah Jacobsson Purewal noted in *PC World*, with Timeline it takes only a few clicks to see data that previously required around 500 clicks on the link labelled "older posts", each click separated by a few seconds delay while the next batch of data loads. Purewal provides a step-by-step guide to reasserting privacy under the new timeline regime, the steps are numerous and the ultimate conclusion is that "you may want to just consider getting rid of your Facebook account and starting from scratch". Though admittedly not scientific, a poll by Sophos, an IT security and data protection company, showed that over half those polled were worried about Timeline. The survey included over 4,000 Facebook users from a population that is likely both more concerned and more knowledgeable about privacy and security than the average user. If that wasn't telling enough, the author of the announcement, Sophos' senior technology consultant, Graham Cluley, announced in the same article that he had shutdown his Facebook account. Cluley's reasoning was a response to realizing exactly how much of his personal data Facebook was holding, and fatigue at Facebook's ever changing and non-consultative privacy regime.

All accounts have both a breadth and a depth. Accounts that are identity-verified, frequently updated, and used across multiple aspects of a person's life present the richest data and pose the greatest risk. The concept of a government-issued national identity card has created fierce debate in many countries, yet that debate has been muted when the data is collected and held by non-government actors. Google's new ubiquitous account and Facebook's single platform for all forms of social communication should raise similar concerns for individuals as both consumers and citizens. . . .

Privacy and Caveat Emptor

In discussing the ethics of social science research, [Constance] Holden noted two schools of thought: utilitarianism (also known as consequentialism) holds that an act can only be judged on its consequences; deontologicalism (also known as non-consequentialism) is predominantly about absolute moral ethics. In the 1960s utilitarianism was dominant, along with moral relativism; in the late 1970s deontologicalism began to hold sway. In computational social science, the debate seems to be academic with little regard given to ethics. Conditions of use are typically one-sided without user input, although Wikipedia is a notable exception. Companies expand their services and data sets with little regard for ethical considerations, and market forces in the form of user backlashes [are] the first, and often only, line of resistance.

One such backlash occurred over Facebook's Beacon software, which was eventually cancelled as part of an out of court settlement. Beacon connected people's purchases to their Facebook account; it advertised to their friends what a user had purchased, where they got it, and whether they got a discount. In one instance, a wife found out about a surprise Christmas gift of jewellery after her husband's purchase was broadcast to all his friends—including his wife. Others found their video rentals widely shared, raising concerns it might out people's sexual preferences and other details of their private life. In addition to closing down Beacon, the settlement involved the establishment of a fund to better study privacy issues, an indication that progress was stepping well ahead of ethical considerations.

The *caveat emptor* view of responsibility for disclosure of personal data by social networking sites is arguably unsustainable. Through Beacon, retailers shared purchasing information with Facebook based on terms and conditions purchasers either failed to notice, or failed to fully appreciate. Beacon took transactions outside consumers' reasonable expectations. While

Facebook was forced to discontinue the service, appropriate ethical consideration by technology professionals could have highlighted the problems at a much earlier stage.

2

People Are Willing to Trade Less Privacy for Access to Social Media

Kent Anderson

Kent Anderson is the chief executive officer and publisher of the Journal of Bone & Joint Surgery. *Prior to this, he was an executive at the* New England Journal of Medicine *and the director of medical journals at the American Academy of Pediatrics.*

Facebook's business model relies on sharing information about its users, and over time it has offered users less and less privacy. Critics have argued that Facebook is cynical and even evil and that it is deliberately eroding social norms around the issue of privacy. However, social networks are based on sharing information, so anyone using such a network is automatically accepting infringements on privacy. Facebook may simply be recognizing that participation in social networks requires people to give up some privacy.

Privacy has become the watchword in social networking. We all worry about an invasion of our privacy, usually thought of as a direct release of confidential information or an indirect insight garnered by concatenating [linking together] a lot of little separate pieces of information about us (e.g., knowing when to rob our house by noting travel plans or location of tweets).

Kent Anderson, "Is Facebook Eroding Privacy? Or Does Social Media Require Us to Lower Our Expectations?" *Scholarly Kitchen*, May 10, 2010. Copyright © 2010 by Kent Anderson. All rights reserved. Reproduced by permission.

Diminishing Privacy

Facebook is no stranger to privacy complaints. Despite its checkered past and flashpoint status, Facebook has no choice but to continue to test the boundaries of privacy—its business model depends on people divulging things about themselves. Its privacy policies have been gradually shifting, in ways users realize and in ways users don't quite see or understand.

As an Electronic Frontier Foundation (EFF) post detailing the timeline of Facebook privacy policies concludes:

> . . . the successive policies tell a clear story. Facebook originally earned its core base of users by offering them simple and powerful controls over their personal information. As Facebook grew larger and became more important, it could have chosen to maintain or improve those controls. Instead, it's slowly but surely helped itself—and its advertising and business partners—to more and more of its users' information, while limiting the users' options to control their own information.

Critics point out that Facebook itself is a major force in changing [the] social norms in its efforts to erode privacy to drive its business.

Recently, Facebook announced the Open Graph Protocol, which makes it easier for outside sites to share information with Facebook when visitors want to recommend a page.

On the heels of this new initiative, *Technology Review* interviewed Danah Boyd of Microsoft Research New England. Boyd is a social media researcher and a vocal critic of Facebook's approach to privacy.

Facebook argues that social norms are changing, and the old definitions of privacy are outdated. Critics point out that Facebook itself is a major force in changing these social norms in its efforts to erode privacy to drive its business. As Boyd says:

I think the social norms have not changed. I think they're being battered by the way the market forces are operating at this point. I think the market is pushing people in a direction that has huge consequences, especially for those who are marginalized.

We all inhabit multiple roles in life—employee, researcher, parent, spouse, child, friend, neighbor—and what may be fine in one role (sharing a long night with friends over drinks) may look completely inappropriate when seen by people expecting you to fulfill another role (boss, parent, spouse). Erosion of privacy erodes the bulwarks we expect between these, and that can make us nervous or prove embarrassing or awkward.

We've all seen religious, political, or social views of old friends and co-workers revealed on Facebook despite the fact that these views have never mattered to our relationships with these people and, worse, may make it harder to look at those people the same way afterward. You can't unlearn the fact that Person A was just revealed as a Scientologist [a religion with controversial beliefs], for example.

As Boyd notes, it's especially bad for teachers:

[Teachers] have a role to play during the school day and there are times and places where they have lives that are not student-appropriate. Online, it becomes a different story. Facebook has now made it so that you can go and see everybody's friends regardless of how private your profile is. And the teachers are constantly struggling with the fact that, no matter how obsessively they've tried to make their profiles as private as possible, one of their friends can post a photo from when they were 16 and drinking or doing something else stupid, and all of a sudden, kids bring it into school.

Some reactions to these perceptions of privacy erosion are stronger than others. Some critics urge others to dump Facebook specifically, and accuse Facebook of nearly evil behavior.

Business Insider has a list of 10 Reasons to Delete Your Facebook Account. They include:

- Facebook's Terms of Service are completely one-sided

- Facebook's CEO has a documented history of unethical behavior

- Facebook has flat-out declared war on privacy

The essential message from the full list is that Facebook is trying to redefine privacy to suit its purposes—commercial purposes based on a plan to become the dominant force online.

Lowering Expectations

Expectations for privacy are very high among the critics of Facebook. As Thomas Baekdal stated in his first rule of privacy:

I am the only one who can decide what I want to share.

In light of this very simple and reasonable rule, it's tempting (and perhaps too easy) to say that these social networks must reflect social expectations and norms as they exist, and not try to shift them to suit their engineering preferences, business models, or tin-eared anthems of social media utopianism.

However, a recent paper in arXiv calculates a mathematical threshold of privacy for social recommendation engines, one that is probably lower than current social norms would accept. The authors believe their calculations indicate a fundamental limit on privacy in social networks, and show that the more people and recommendations that are present, the more this threshold moves toward a lack of privacy. In other words, to get social recommendations, we have to give up some of our privacy—and the more people who share and seek social recommendations, the less privacy there is. As the authors state it:

> This finding throws into serious question the feasibility of developing social recommendation algorithms that are both accurate and privacy-preserving for many real-world settings.

Facebook is a flashpoint among social networks—being the leader, it's on the forefront of criticism. But if this recent paper is correct, the genre itself may demand a change in social expectations of privacy among users. It may not be Facebook's fault or Mark Zuckerberg's business cynicism at work. It may be reality, and the critics may just be scapegoating Facebook.

Perhaps Facebook's sense of shifting social norms is right, informed by years of watching a major social network blossom around them. The trade-off their observations might have identified could be: If people continue to use and rely upon social networks, they are implicitly accepting a lower threshold of privacy.

3

Social Media Helps to Fuel Political Reform

Serajul I. Bhuiyan

Serajul I. Bhuiyan is an associate professor and program director in the Department of Mass Communications and Journalism at Texas A&M University-Texarkana.

In 2011, Egyptians staged protests against an authoritarian regime and unseated President Hosni Mubarek. The revolution was enabled in many ways by social media, which allowed people to connect with one another, organize, and (via YouTube especially) share images of repression and protest with the world. While social media may not have directly caused the revolution, its importance can be seen by the fact that, during the protests, the government tried to shut down all social media platforms. The success of the revolution demonstrates that social media can be a great force for democracy.

As countries around the world discover the influence of social media, citizens have begun to use its power to better their lives; one such country, Egypt, has created a new standard for social reform through social media and networking. Egypt possesses a long and rich history, a cohesive kingdom from around 3200 B.C. Over thousands of years, various nations ruled Egypt; in 1952, it finally gained independence from outside rulers, ousting the British-backed monarchy. Since then Egypt has been a republic, and until the revolution

Serajul I. Bhuiyan, "Social Media and Its Effectiveness in the Political Reform Movement in Egypt," *Middle East Media Educator* 1:1, 2011, pp. 14–20. Copyright © 2011 by Middle East Media Educator. All rights reserved. Reproduced by permission.

of 2011, was ruled by President Hosni Mubarak who had attempted to reform Egypt's slow economy by decentralizing it; however, that didn't work, and Egypt's citizens remain poor, 20 percent living below poverty level. The country ranks 21st in the world for Internet users, with just over 20 million users in 2009 out of a population of 83 million or roughly one quarter. This is surprising if one considers the Internet a vital instrument in the Egyptian revolt.

Giving People a Voice

Social media and networking have come to define a new generation of communication and have created a platform that possesses limitless abilities to connect, share, and explore our world. Social media is not a new idea, however; people have used technology for decades now to communicate, mobilize voters for political participation and, "while it has only recently become part of mainstream culture and the business world, people have been using digital media for networking, socializing and information gathering—almost exactly like now—for over 30 years."

> Social media did not cause Egypt's revolution; however, it accelerated the movement.

Social media is content created and shared by individuals on the web using available websites which allow members of the site to create and display their photos, thoughts, and videos. Social media allows people to share content with a select group or with everyone. Social media is a way for communicating with one or more people at the same time. Using these sites allows people to communicate in real-time and thereby is effective in developing democracy because social media sites give people a voice to express their opinions about government, television, political leaders, and any other issues of concern. Sites like Twitter, Facebook, and YouTube allow power to be shifted to people. They create two-way communication between individuals or small groups and the general public.

Causes of Egypt's Revolution

During Egypt's modern period from the revolution of 1952 to the present, there have been struggles at the top of government, but only recently has the popular outcry for social reform become visible. In 1981, Egypt's leader Anwar Sadat was assassinated, bringing President Mubarak into power. Mubarak ruled with an autocratic style, and continued to enforce the Emergency Law 30 years after Sadat's assassination. The Emergency Law "allows police to arrest people without charge, detain prisoners indefinitely, limit freedom of expression and assembly, and maintain a special security court."

Although the law supposedly applied mainly to drug trafficking and terrorism, it was abused so greatly that the government's promise to use it sparingly proved meaningless, angering Egypt's population. In 2010, people's grievances grew exponentially as multiple problems with security, terrorism, and the economy worsened. On January 25, 2011, Egyptians took to the streets in Cairo, Alexandria, and some other places in the so-called Day of Revolt, concentrating their grievances on legal and political matters. Rather than a typical small protest, the Day of Revolt exploded into a monumental moment in Egypt's history because of social media. Social media did not cause Egypt's revolution; however, it accelerated the movement. Viral videos, such as [Egyptian activist] Asmaa Mahfouz's, and the [protest] suicide of [street vendor] Mohamed Bouazizi in Tunisia created a surge of emotion in Egyptians, persuading them to protest.

Egyptian protestors used Facebook and Twitter to get people out on the streets within the country and YouTube to let the world know what was happening. By using tools that the regime underestimated, activists were able to spread hope, not only to Egyptians, but also worldwide, encouraging other repressed populations to attempt something similar in their countries. Because of the protests, President Mubarak stepped down and turned his power over to the Supreme Council of the Armed Forces; however, at the time of publication [2011], protests continue in an effort to speed the process of what many Egyptians see as extinguishing the last remnants of the old regime. Without social media allowing Egyptians to communicate with the outside world, the government would have been able to quickly suppress the protests.

The people of Egypt were influenced by the earlier revolution in Tunisia where thousands of people protested unemployment, government corruption, and poverty by taking over the streets. The Tunisian revolution and its success in eliminating the long time leader caught the attention of Egyptians facing similar issues. Egyptians wanted change in their country and the elimination of President Mubarak who had been in power for 30 years. Social media sites helped spark and organize the first protest on January 25, 2011, which 85,000 people had pledged on Facebook to attend. When the government used force, the situation gained international attention on Twitter and YouTube. We must remember, however, that without the perseverance of the Egyptian people, the revolution would have never happened, leaving the question: To what extent does social media affect revolution in Egypt?

The economic and social situation is dire. On April 22, 2011, the US dollar is equivalent to approximately six Egyptian pounds (EGP). Wages are approximately 35 EGP per month for most people, and 289 EPG for government employees and sector workers, meaning 6 USD and 48 USD respectively. [Economist] Fatah El-Gebali is quoted as saying, "There is a big problem in reaching a consensus on the issue. The trade unions want to set the minimum wage around 1,200 Egyptian pounds (200 USD) per month, while business associations want a maximum of 400 Egyptian Pounds (67 USD)." The fairest minimum wage, based on a 25 percent per capita of GNP, appears to be around 733 EGP (122 USD). At that rate, economist Samir Radawan states, "the share of those who would receive the minimum wage is not significant enough to have a dent on inflation." Current minimum wages have not increased since 1984 although inflation has.

Malcom Gladwell believes that the influence of social media is limited, and the revolutions would have happened anyway.

According to statistics from the CIA (2011): the unemployment rate was 9.4 percent in 2009 and 9.7 percent in 2010; population below poverty level was 20 percent; inflation was 11.9 percent in 2009 and 12.8 percent in 2010; in 2010 the budget showed revenue of 46 billion and 64 billion expenditures; the debt rose from 29.66 billion to 30.61 billion in the year from 2009–2010; and in 2010 imports were nearly double exports. The literacy rate is quite low according to the CIA with around 83 percent male and 59.4 percent female literacy rates in 2005; in 2008 3.8 percent of the nation's gross profit went toward education. The mean age of citizens is 24 years of age; therefore, the majority of the citizens are likely to be aware of the media around them and thus likely to be knowledgeable about the impact of the economic situation on their future.

Role of Social Media in the Revolution

Philip Howard quoted an activist in Cairo as saying, "We use Facebook to schedule the protests, Twitter to coordinate, and YouTube to tell the world." This statement sums up the use of social media in the protest. . . .

Newsweek calls it the Facebook Revolt; in fact, it could also be called the Twitter Revolution, the first of its kind. However, not everyone agrees with the Facebook Revolution concept. Malcom Gladwell believes that the influence of social media is limited, and the revolutions would have happened anyway; "I mean, in cases where there are no tools of communication, people still get together. So I don't see that as being . . . in looking at history, I don't see the absence of efficient tools of communication as being a limiting factor on the ability of people to socially organize."

Gladwell is correct that the revolution would have happened without social media because revolutions happened in the past when the internet didn't exist; however, the revolution probably would not have happened as soon, and probably would not have sparked as quickly as it did. People were able to coordinate protests and bring out larger numbers because of Facebook and Twitter, and they were able to show what actually was happening, and counter government attempts to play down the situation because of YouTube. Social media also shaped the way the world viewed the protests. For instance, an Egyptian blogger stated, "I urge you to use the words 'revolt' and 'uprising' and 'revolution' and not 'chaos' and not 'unrest.' We are talking about a historic moment." Shortly after CNN changed a headline from "CHAOS IN EGYPT" to "UPRISING IN EGYPT."

Obviously, the Egyptian government that was being overthrown agreed that social media was significant because it tried to block the key sites. This is confirmed by a tweet from twitterglobalpr: "We can confirm that Twitter was blocked in Egypt around 8am [January 25th]. It is impacting both Twitter.com and applications. We believe that the open exchange of info and views benefits societies and helps [governments] better connect [with] their people."

Also confirmed were blocking of Facebook, MySpace, YouTube, and mobile phones. Ungeleider reports that people in Tahrir Square were unlocking their WiFi signals to allow for mobile phones to get around the blocks; proxy servers were also used which change the URL to hide which site is being surfed. There are too many proxies to block them all.

ALLEN PARK PUBLIC LIBRARY #4

Social Media on the Rise in Egypt

Social media allowed Egyptians living under dictatorship to communicate with the world. Egyptians used Facebook, Twitter, and YouTube to send millions of internet links, news, articles, videos, and free campaigns to people all over the world. The internet allowed people living in a state that controlled traditional media to complain about conditions. News quickly spread because Twitter allowed Egyptians to upload information as it happened and write comments about their government. This helped to gain national attention because Egyptians wanted change for their country. Social media allowed the free speech that wasn't allowed by the government.

Eighteen days after the protests began in Tahrir Square and elsewhere, Egyptians finally shouted victory. They had joined together to defeat the government with the help of social media.

Facebook helped to get the messages out to the world about the devastation that was occurring in Egypt through photos and videos. An Egyptian named Khaled Said was killed after he posted a video of police officers engaging in illegal activity. The photos of the dead man on Facebook were so gruesome that they angered Egyptians tired of brutality, immoral arrest, and crooked government. Shortly after, Wael Ghonim created a Facebook page titled "We Are All Khaled Said." That Facebook page gained 500,000 members. This led to Ghonim's being captured, blindfolded, and detained for 10 days. Ghonim who later became the symbol of Egypt's pro-democracy tweeted "Freedom is a bless[ing] that deserves fighting for." This motivated thousands of Egyptians who agreed to keep protesting. As the protests continued, more people in Egypt turned to Facebook to see videos, pictures, make comments, and discuss the political revolution for democracy, freedom of speech, and socio-economic change. . . .

Videos on YouTube showed thousands of people marching, fighting, and running from tear gas. It was a battle for justice that was captured on YouTube for the world to see. Protestors were shot, hit with rocks, run over by vans, and killed by police officers. YouTube was the social medium that captured the action of the 18-day Revolution. People chanted, "Don't leave until [Mubarak] leaves," and held sit-ins. The videos gave international exposure to the violence. YouTube also allowed subscribers to comment on the videos. One subscriber stated, "I'm Egyptian, I'm 20 years old and I saw no hope, no future, no justice, nothing. . . . God bless everyone who sacrificed their lives for us to lead a better life. . . ." This is just one example of how a single thought that expresses a person's feelings can be read around the world. YouTube established a democracy where everyone is able to express an opinion through the internet.

The Government Tries to Fight Back

With the uproar of the social media, more people began expressing themselves in a society where it was uncommon. To retaliate, the government decided to shut down all social media sites to prevent interaction with other nations. On January 29, 2011, Twitter and other social media sites were blocked. The government must have thought that this move would stop the protests. However, the Egyptian Revolution was a key interest on social media sites that captured the attention of a lot of people. Egypt remained a trending topic on Twitter even while the site was blocked in Egypt.

When the government disabled social media sites, Habib Haddad created an alternative to help spread the message. He teamed with Google and Twitter and found at least 1,000 translators who translated Arabic tweets into French, German, and English. This gave people in other countries a way to continue to communicate with Egyptians and to stay informed about what was happening. The application was called

Speak2Tweet, and it allowed people to leave voice messages that were posted to Twitter. On February 11, 2011, known as Farewell Friday, Hosni Mubarak stepped down after 30 years. Eighteen days after the protests began in Tahrir Square and elsewhere, Egyptians finally shouted victory. They had joined together to defeat the government with the help of social media.

The new revolution in social media has exploded into an effective tool of communication, not only to connect socially, but also to ignite political reform and social action. Perhaps social media was not absolutely critical to the uprising in Egypt; however, it made protest possible sooner, and helped it develop in a way that would have been impossible without social media. Looking at the impact of Facebook here in America, I see that people ask for a Facebook profile instead of a telephone number; they chat online instead of talking on the phone; emailing has started to decline compared to increasing use of social media and blogging. Around the world social media has opened new possibilities for communication and social change.

4

Authoritarian Regimes Use Social Networks for Repression

Joel Simon

Joel Simon is the executive director of the Committee to Protect Journalists.

Social media and the Internet can be used by advocates of democracy but they can also be used by authoritarian governments to shut down dissent. For example, Cuba and Burma prevent most of their population from going online. China and Iran block and monitor certain content and arrest and imprison bloggers or individuals who violate the bans. In order to defend journalism, therefore, it is important to defend the Internet itself from interference. Businesses, governments, and advocacy organizations must work together to prevent repressive regimes from turning the Internet and social media into tools of repression rather than freedom.

In what has been dubbed "The Twitter Revolution," citizens in Tehran since June [2009] have been documenting violence in the street and using social media to disseminate information to fellow protesters as well as an eager audience around the word. Their efforts bolster the idea that the Internet cannot be controlled, and that even the most repressive and determined government cannot stop the flow of information.

Joel Simon, "Repression Goes Digital," *Columbia Journalism Review*, March 30, 2010. Copyright © 2010 by Joel Simon. All rights reserved. Reproduced by permission.

The Internet and Repression

This is an appealing and exciting notion, one touted by many Iran watchers, but it ignores the fuller and more ominous reality of the cat and mouse game unfolding between journalists—professional and amateur—and those repressive regimes in Iran and elsewhere. Yes, Twitter and e-mail have made it possible to get fragmented bits of information out of Iran, but the hard-line government in Tehran may be winning the information war by forcing foreign correspondents out of the country or keeping them in their bureaus, shutting down reformist newspapers, rounding up critical bloggers and journalists, and, on occasion, disabling the Internet and cell service entirely.

Beyond that, the situation in Iran points to serious vulnerabilities in the global information environment that have broad implications for journalism and press freedom: as more and more media outlets converge online, the Internet is becoming an information chokepoint that governments are seeking to control.

Pulling the plug on the Internet is an extreme measure, although Iran has done it for brief periods and China essentially shut down the Internet for months in Xinjiang province to prevent coverage of the unrest there. But governments from Tunisia to Vietnam are using monitors, filters, firewalls, and pressure on service providers to gain control of the Internet and stem the flow of information. In recent examples, government hackers have taken down critical Web Sites in Russia and Tunisia. Governments are also jailing critical bloggers, who are vulnerable because, unlike professional journalists, they generally lack institutional backing.

In seeking to stem the flow of information online, governments have exploited vulnerabilities at each step in the journalism process: the gathering, dissemination, and consumption of news.

Before the Internet, news gatherers were mostly professional journalists. Over decades, governments around the world developed refined if imperfect strategies to control their activities, from denying visas and accreditation to the threat of prison sentences and even murder. But the Web changed the equation, since nearly everyone now has the capacity to gather and disseminate information using e-mail, the Web, social networking platforms, and, increasingly, SMS [short message service] networks like Twitter. The sheer number of potential news gatherers presents new challenges to governments trying to stop information at its source. Iranian security forces, for instance, have made haphazard efforts to physically attack protesters who are using cell phones to document abuses. They are also attempting to use technology to suppress news gathering. According to media reports, Nokia Siemens, a Finnish-German joint venture, has sold Iran technology that allows authorities to monitor any communications across a network, including voice calls, text messaging, instant messages, and Web traffic. (The company says it provided only "Lawful Intercept capacity solely for the monitoring of local voice calls in Iran.") The Iranian government also set up a Web site asking people to help identify photos of protesters and turn them in.

The simplest way to stop the dissemination of information or ideas is to limit access to the Internet or cellular networks.

If repressive governments cannot effectively control the information gatherers, they must either prevent them from disseminating the information or stop news consumers from accessing it. In both areas, governments have had surprising success. Their job is made easier by the fact that more and more information, whether collected by professional journalists or average citizens, is disseminated through the Web.

Keep People Off-Line

The simplest way to stop the dissemination of information or ideas is to limit access to the Internet or cellular networks. This is a strategy employed in some of the world's most repressive countries, such us Burma and Cuba. By making it difficult for average citizens to get online, these governments inhibit the rise of mass citizen journalism, and make it easy to target the individuals who defy the government.

Burma, which was named the world's worst place to be a blogger in a 2009 survey by the Committee to Protect Journalists (CPJ), broadly restricts Internet access, forcing people to access the Web through cyber cafés, which are carefully monitored. Bloggers caught disseminating damaging information have been severely punished. The comedian Muang Thura, for instance (better known as Zarganar, or "tweezers"), is serving a thirty-five-year sentence for distributing video of relief workers assisting the victims of Cyclone Nargis.

In Cuba, Internet access is officially restricted to government officials and members of the Communist Party, but a handful of independent bloggers operate in the country, using Internet cafés to access the Web. For the most part, Cuban authorities tolerate this because the bloggers don't directly challenge the government and because their work is generally available only outside the island.

Limiting Information

Blocking or severely limiting access to the Web, however, comes with a high economic and political cost. Governments that don't let their citizens online are among the world's most repressive; increasingly, a country cannot be part of the global economy without an information-based society. Countries like China and Iran take a more sophisticated approach, allowing broad access to the Internet but limiting the dissemination of certain kinds of critical content. This requires manpower and technology. In China, for example, an army of tens of thousands of Internet monitors scrutinizes the Web and removes "objectionable" content. The government blocks individual Web sites and key-word searches, monitors the use of certain terms ("Falun Gong," "Tiananmen Square"),[1] and arrests those who post commentary critical of the regime. In one recent case, the dissident poet Liu Xiaobo was sentenced on Christmas Day to eleven years in prison for "inciting subversion of state power."

The big fear of press-freedom advocates is creeping censorship under the guise of law enforcement or anti-pornography legislation.

But China also understands that broad Web and cellular access—China has more online users than any other country—is necessary for global business. Most Chinese citizens operate happily inside a "walled garden," where they are permitted to peruse a variety of information and even post certain kinds of critical comments. According to Rebecca MacKinnon, a China expert who is writing a book on the subject, most people in China lack the technical means or even the interest to access blocked news sites, like the BBC Chinese service, or YouTube. China is also putting pressure on the Internet Service Providers (ISPs), requiring them to serve as surrogate censors.

Iranians, too, have had broad access to the Web, a technology that has been embraced by the country's conservative leadership, many of whom host blogs and Twitter. But Iran's Internet connection to the World is in the hands of Telecommunications Company of Iran, a company in which a consortium associated with the Revolutionary Guards recently bought a 50 percent stake. Cyrus Farivar, a San Francisco-based tech journalist and Iran expert, calls control of the In-

---

1. Falun Gong is a spiritual practice that China has outlawed. Tiananmen Square refers to a failed protest movement in China in 1989.

ternet "the biggest weapon in the government's arsenal." The number of international gateways that allow Internet traffic to enter or exit Iran is in the "single digits," according to Farivar.

Restrictions of online content are not limited to repressive countries. Germany, for example, bans Holocaust deniers and neo-Nazis and requires Internet companies like Google and Yahoo to comply with government regulations. In India, according to a recent piece in *The Wall Street Journal*, Google has been forced to remove or censor content that could offend religious minorities or powerful political figures. The big fear of press-freedom advocates is creeping censorship under the guise of law enforcement or anti-pornography legislation.

Governments can also attack the third part of the information assembly line, blocking people from accessing certain kinds of information on the Web. Many repressive governments—including Iran, Tunisia, Saudi Arabia, Ethiopia, and China—use filters to block critical Web sites, a process known as blacklisting. Whitelisting, which is also widely practiced, refers to authorizing approved Web sites and blocking the rest. Increasingly, governments also require Internet café owners to police the sites that their clients visit; some have installed software that allows the government to do this remotely.

Defend the Internet

Press freedom groups like CPJ [Committee to Protect Journalists] have traditionally focused their attention on defending news gatherers. These strategies remain crucial, but in order to more effectively defend press freedom in the new global information environment we need to devote more resources to defending the Internet itself. CPJ, for example, is adding a full-time Internet advocacy coordinator in 2010 to do just that. Our goal is to get media organizations to understand that they have an enormous stake in the outcome.

To be effective, journalists, media organizations, and press-freedom groups need to form alliances with the ISPs and tech companies that maintain the Internet's infrastructure. These companies are coming under tremendous pressure from repressive governments to enforce government censorship. Too often they have complied and have been justly criticized for doing so.

Governments . . . have a role to play in defending press freedom online.

That is why Google's recent stand in China is so important. Refusing to comply with Chinese government censorship "was a statement that doing the moral and ethical thing is good for business," says Rebecca MacKinnon. "When your business is transmitting, publishing, amplifying, and hosting the most intimate details of people's lives and their most sensitive political conversations, then your users have to trust that you're not going to be tossing information to the nearest dictator."

Good for business, but also good for journalism. However, these kinds of efforts will only be effective if companies agree to abide by minimum standards that prevent competitors from exploiting another's principled position. A new organization called the Global Network Initiative was set up to do that. The organization, which expects to hire an executive director in the next few months, is made up of leading Internet companies—Google, Yahoo, and Microsoft—along with human rights organizations and socially responsible investors. Robert Mahoney, CPJ's deputy director, represents us on the initiative's board.

A united front has proved effective, as was shown last summer when international tech companies forced the Chinese government to back away from its plan to require the installation of filtering software called Green Dam/Youth Escort in every computer sold in China.

Governments, too, have a role to play in defending press freedom online. "We stand for a single Internet, where all of humanity has equal access to knowledge and ideas," Secretary of State Hillary Clinton noted in a January [2010] speech at the Newseum in Washington, D.C. Turning that lofty rhetoric into effective policy will be a major challenge.

The goal of everyone fighting for press freedom on the Internet is to bring together journalists, ISPs, tech and media companies, freedom of expression and human rights groups, and even supportive governments in a broad international coalition to preserve and strengthen Internet freedom and push back against countries that seek to restrict it. The future of free journalism may depend on the success of this coalition.

Technology will play a role, but it's only one tool. Equally important is consistent public pressure on governments that employ censorship. The perception that dissident voices rather than repressive governments have benefited more from the advent of the Internet is probably correct—but only for the moment. As MacKinnon notes, "The Internet is an extension of human activity, and secret police and criminals have moved into cyberspace along with the wonderful democracy activists we all like."

5

Social Networks Change Government in Numerous Ways, for Good and Ill

Alexander B. Howard

Alexander B. Howard is a writer and editor and a former Washington, DC, correspondent for O'Reilly Media.

The shift to Web 2.0, or the widespread use of social media, has affected the way that governments interact with their citizens. Greater connections tend to create more possibilities for collaboration and shift power away from centralized authorities. In the United States, social media has been used by citizens to follow political debates and to express their opinions to congressmen and women and to congressional staffers. It has also been used by the president to encourage citizen feedback and participation. Social media has become an important channel for communication between people and their representatives, and it may be influencing debate in new and important ways.

*T*his is all part of a historic continuum, as Adam Conner, Facebook's first staffer in Washington, D.C., reflected in an essay shared with this correspondent.

When the use of the telephone became widespread, the ability to establish instantaneous audio communication between two separate points was a game-changer for government agencies. They no longer needed to rely solely on in-

Alexander B. Howard, "How Governments Deal With Social Media," *National Journal*, August 9, 2011. Copyright © 2011 by Alexander B. Howard. All rights reserved. Reproduced by permission.

person meetings or written correspondence for communication and operations and service became many times faster, more efficient and more personal.

We believe that social media can be similarly transformative to the way government and constituents interact. While it is possible in the first years of a new communication technology to delegate responsibility and knowledge to a few individuals, as adoption grows, it becomes impossible, impractical, and inefficient to silo that knowledge in one place. This was definitely true of the telephone.

The telephone shifted the way that everyone in the government conducted business on a daily basis. It didn't just affect GS-8 level "Telephone Specialist" government employees. Inevitably, everyone had to have a phone and know how to use one. Understanding how to use phones, email, social media, and the next big thing won't be a requirement—it'll be so expected that to encounter someone who doesn't will give you genuine pause.

Today, there are still people who install and repair phones but there's no one around who teaches you to pick up the phone when it makes a noise and say hello. In the same way, the duties of "Online Communication Specialist" and "New Media Director" are important and their work will continue for years to come. But these specialized jobs related to using a new technology will eventually fade away as they are integrated into the broader areas they fill. And the title "New Media Director" may become as commonplace as "Director of Two-Way Wirebound Audio Communication."

Editor's Note: For good or for ill, governments have to deal with social media. In Cairo and London and Washington, the way people organize themselves is changing—and governments are struggling to adapt, adopt, co-opt, or disable the technologies that enable these changes. Here, O'Reilly Media's Government 2.0 correspondent takes a step back and surveys the landscape at the crossroads of social media and political power in the summer of 2011.

In the 1990s, the Internet changed communication and commerce forever. A decade later, the Web 2.0 revolution created a new disruption, enabling hundreds of millions of citizens to publish, share, mix, comment, and upload media to a more dynamic online environment. That two-way communication, enabled by new, highly accessible and scalable Web technologies, is generally called "social media." In the years since the first social networks went online, the disruption has spread to government, creating shifts in power structures as large as those enabled by the introduction of the printing press centuries ago.

"Connection technologies, including social media, tend to devolve power from the nation state and large institutions to individuals and small institutions," Alec J. Ross, senior innovation adviser to Secretary of State Hillary Clinton, said in an interview. "Nothing demonstrated that more than the power to publish and distribute at great scale by historically disempowered individuals with inexpensive devices."

For a recent example, consider the role of social media in revolutions in Tunisia and Egypt, where YouTube, Facebook, and Twitter acted in combination with Al Jazeera and mobile phones to catalyze reactions to deep-seated repression. "If governments are not engaging in social media, they are essentially ceding influence and power," said Ross.

It also provides new capabilities and opportunities to work with the public in collaboration, co-creation or oversight. Social media is changing how state and local government elections are covered, including fraud or corruption reporting. In California, social media is connecting citizens to e-services, and it is an elemental component of New York's bid to be the nation's premier digital city. In Washington and other capitals around the world, legislatures and executive offices now operate in a 24-hour stream of live updates and discussion. This

January, the Congressional transition was streamed live online, as well as on Twitter and Facebook. After President Obama's historic speech on Middle East policy, the White House turned to Twitter to discuss it.

"Social media allows for more distributed communication and collaboration when natural or man-made crises occur," said Ross. "This allows for faster and more inclusive, broadly participatory responses to life and death situations." For example, in Australia, social media and geospatial mapping helped crisis responders deal with historic floods. In San Francisco, city services, 311 and Facebook are enabling new ways of solving civic issues.

Mainstream media is increasingly merging with social media. Last year, more citizens experienced "Twitter TV" during sporting events like the World Cup. This fall, Facebook and NBC will co-host the Republican primary debate. (Don't get lost in the glitz of social media, though: Election 2012 will be about the data.) In June 2011, Google launched YouTube for Government, offering civic leaders around the world a platform to reach all connected citizens.

Social media does present novel risks and rewards for government beyond the changes wrought by telegraph, telephone, and television. Social media creates new online privacy challenges for citizens and government alike. It presents a real headache for the government employees entrusted with records management. A recent GAO report highlighted the need for consistent social media policies that address security, privacy, and records keeping.

Under repressive governments and autocracies, social media can act as a tool of oppression as well as freedom. Congress faces challenges in identifying constituents using social media. That said, the Internet has become the public arena for our time. One challenge is that third-party platforms control this 21st-century public square, creating novel issues for government's relationship with the technology companies that host civic dialogue.

After the president and House speaker addressed the nation on the debt crisis and called for public support, House and Senate websites were swamped with electronic interest. Many citizens turned to Facebook and Twitter to contact congressional staffers on social media expecting to be heard.

The White House has turned to social media to advocate for #compromise, starting with a tweet from the president himself on his campaign account. The subsequent ripple of feedback suggested the influence of political communication over social networks. Statistics provided via e-mail by Twitter government liaison Adam Sharp offer more data about Twitter: "Tweets regarding #debt & related keywords peaked two times" during the last week of the debt ceiling debate, according to Sharp, driven by Monday's primetime speeches and Friday's "Call to Tweet." Further, Sharp wrote that @mentions of members of Congress increased three times from Friday over Thursday, a five-fold increase over the previous week's average. White House communications director Dan Pfeiffer affirmed to *New York Times* reporter Brian Stelter that e-mail and tweets from constituents influenced Sunday's debt ceiling deal, along with phone calls. Fittingly, perhaps, the interaction between the two men happened over social media.

During these dog days of summer, we've also seen massive dissatisfaction with elected representatives expressed by citizens using social media, including the anti-Washington hashtag Jeff Jarvis started during the debt-ceiling debate. Social media platforms will continue to reflect both that tension and a reality. While technology empowers citizens to have a real-time conversation with their governments, the men and women entrusted with making laws and policies will find better ways to govern amid the tumult. Congressional staffers are on social media but, as Nick Clark Judd pointed out, "it bears mentioning that the conversation that congressional staffers are listening to on social media is the same one they've been in for years."

Whether or not social media played a critical role in the debt ceiling debate, Middle East revolutions or the 2008 and 2010 elections, one truth has become even more clear in the summer of 2011: these channels now complement the use of phone, email, texts and television in the business of government, and they're not going away.

6

Social Networking Is Addictive and Can Lead to Psychological Disorders

Larry D. Rosen, Nancy A. Cheever, and L. Mark Carrier

Larry D. Rosen is professor and past chair of the psychology department at California State University, Dominguez Hills. Nancy A. Cheever is an associate professor of communications at California State University, Dominguez Hills, and a media psychology research consultant with RCC Consulting Group. L. Mark Carrier is professor of psychology at California State University, Dominguez Hills.

Internet and social media addiction can be a serious problem. The need to continually play games, use a smart phone, or use social media can lead to sleep deprivation and can damage real-life relationships with coworkers, friends, or family. Research suggests that Internet addiction may be linked to changes in brain chemistry associated with the rewards of Internet use. However, addiction is also likely linked to social and psychological rewards associated with Internet and social media use.

Jim, a 32-year-old manager at a computer company, cannot leave a room without his Blackberry. At least three or more times a day he pats his pocket to make sure it is there and he

Larry D. Rosen, Nancy A. Cheever, and L. Mark Carrier, *iDisorder: Understanding Our Obsession with Technology and Overcoming Its Hold on Us*. New York, NY: Palgrave Macmillan, 2011. Copyright © 2011 by Palgrave Macmillan. All rights reserved. Reproduced by permission.

checks it all day long. At dinner with his wife and daughter, he has his BlackBerry on the table in front of him, and he spends most of the dinnertime staring at the phone screen.

Hooked on Technology

Jane is hooked on social media. Before she gets out of bed in the morning, she grabs her iPhone from the nightstand and checks for status updates from her friends. Checking Facebook throughout the day is the primary way that she keeps up with her social circle, and she hates having to make phone calls to find out what her friends are up to.

Rick, a 70-year-old grandfather, loves to take photos with his smartphone and then post them online. He especially likes to shoot pictures of his family and then put them online so that distant relatives can see them. He never asks anyone for permission to post the photos publicly despite getting several complaints from family members.

You have heard people talk about friends who they claim are addicted to the Internet and you may have even wondered whether you are addicted. Scientists began developing measurement instruments to identify Internet and technology addicts when stories of such fanatics came to the surface in the mid-1990s. Mostly, these measurement tools are based on several core concepts that come from psychiatrists' and psychologists' understanding of other confirmed addictions, including substance abuse and pathological gambling, both outlined in the *DSM* [Diagnostic and Statistical Manual of Mental Disorders].

Symptoms

Of course, compulsive use is a key part of Internet addiction. An "addict" must overuse the Internet, the cell phone, or other technological devices to be considered abnormal. However, overuse is not the only important part of being addicted to technology, nor is it even a defining feature of addiction. An addict so experiences withdrawal, tolerance, interpersonal and/or health problems, and time management problems. But how do we gauge these experiences when we are dealing with an environment that we all use every day?

An important aspect of technology addiction is that it interferes with "normal" life activities.

Symptoms of withdrawal might include agitation, depression, anger, and anxiety when the person is away from technology or computers. These psychological symptoms might even turn into physical symptoms such as a rapid heartbeat, tense shoulders, and shortness of breath.

And just like with other addictions, technology addiction presents the problem of habituation or tolerance. Tolerance means that an addict grows accustomed to the "high" received from technology use and therefore must do something more extreme to achieve the same high the next time that technology is used. For example, a video game addict could thoroughly enjoy a particular game, but soon he will need to get an even more challenging, more violent, or more interactive game to achieve the same feeling of enjoyment.

As with most iDisorders, an important aspect of technology addiction is that it interferes with "normal" life activities. In other words, just playing lots of video games is not necessarily bad unless playing interferes with one's personal relationships, hygienic behaviors, or work and chores.

Finally, an addict can easily spend more time in technology-based activities than planned. That can result in the addict losing sleep, being late to work or school, and/or skipping face-to-face social activities. . . .

What's Wrong with Overusing the Internet (or Other Technology)?

There are serious negative outcomes that can occur as the result of a technology addiction. Researchers have noted that the consequences of technology addiction are similar to the consequences of chemical addictions such as drugs or alcohol and can include financial problems, job loss, and relationship breakdowns. Kimberly Young provides a case study that demonstrates the financial and relationship problems that can occur as the result of addiction.

Dr. Young's patient, who we will call Jo, described herself as initially computer illiterate, but she became quite enamored with computer use (especially social chat rooms) over time. She began to feel depressed when she wasn't online and, to avoid this, spent more and more time on the computer. She canceled appointments and stopped calling her real-life friends. Significant family problems developed: Her daughters felt ignored and her husband complained about the financial cost of her constant online behavior. She eventually became estranged from her daughters and separated from her husband.

> [Multi-user domains] are addictive because they provide multi-sensory information . . . , realistically portrayed virtual environments, and real-time interaction with other users.

Sleep patterns are often totally disrupted by technology addiction. Technology addicts use their devices or the Internet 40 to 80 hours per week, or they might go on "net binges" in which a single session can last up to 20 hours or more. Given that there are only 168 hours in a week, using technology this much will nearly always result in sleep disruption. Being sleep deprived can impact academic or work performance and even weaken one's immune system. Additionally, sitting around at the computer or on the couch for long periods of time can lead to a loss of exercise, an increased risk of carpal tunnel syndrome, and eye or back strain. For example, a study by the Benesse Institute of Education in Japan found that Japanese youth who used cell phones excessively were likely to come home after midnight and likely to go to bed after one in the morning. They also were more likely than less-frequent cell phone users to be late for school and late for class. In a later study of Japanese youths and cell phone use, it was found that more than one-third of eighth-graders—kids barely out of their preteen years—agreed that cell phone use interferes with their daily schedules. . . .

What's Known About the Biological Basis of Technology Addiction?

Scientists recently began considering whether the brain structures and functions responsible for technology addiction are the same as the ones responsible for classic drug addictions. For drug addictions, much evidence points to an altered reward system in the brain, perhaps involving changes in brain chemical levels (e.g., dopamine and/or serotonin). Recent reviews of the non-substance or behavioral addictions reveal an overlap in the brain circuitry and chemistry with those brain systems involved in substance abuse. Behavioral addictions that have been studied run the gamut from well-investigated ones like gambling addiction to less studied ones like sugar addiction and pornography addiction. The evidence that a behavioral addiction is the same as a drug addiction as far as the brain is concerned appears to be strongest for gambling addictions; however, there is some evidence that Internet addiction might function like a drug addiction. A recent study of brain tissue in adolescents afflicted with Internet addiction leaves no doubt that there are differences between addicts and non-addicts in terms of brain systems. The researchers found that there were significant differences in the gray matter and white matter—measures related to the structure and functions of neurons—between the addicted adolescents, and their "healthy" counterparts.

The Pull of Technology

Technology addiction is probably not just attributable to individuals with certain personality characteristics or brain chemical levels. The technology itself lures us into using it, sometimes for extreme lengths of time. Even when people are not online, they might often be thinking about being online. A relative of mine, Rob, is a 52-year-old father of three boys and consumed by online fantasy football. Rob, who has a very busy job as a contract manager for an international computer consulting firm, provides a good example of the "pull" of technology. When the professional football season starts, Rob becomes obsessed with managing his own fantasy football team. Although football games (real and fantasy) are almost exclusively played on the weekends, the fantasy football website provides plenty of exciting opportunities for checking in and participating during the work week. There are daily posts by sports experts giving advice as to which players should be picked, almost daily "simulations" of head-to-head matchups between players, constantly streaming live "discussions" between fantasy football team owners over who are the best football players, hourly (or faster) news updates about what is happening in the real world of professional football, and a variety of online tools for managing one's own fantasy football team. In other words, there is always something exciting happening online. How can a football fanatic like Rob resist checking in on a frequent basis during the work day, especially when he has a company-issued BlackBerry device that gives him free web access?

As corroboration of Rob's addiction to online fantasy football, Kimberly Young found that interactive programs and software were likely to be linked to Internet dependency. The interactive programs that she observed as critical were Internet chat programs and multi-user domains (MUDs). MUDs are addictive because they provide multi-sensory information (sound and video), realistically portrayed virtual environments, and real-time interaction with other users. Have you ever tried *World of Warcraft*? There is a good chance that you have gone on a quest in this virtual fantasy world given that more than 12 million users were playing it as of 2010. In fact, it is often referred to as *World of Warcrack* because it is so addictive!

Some researchers have likened the sense of excitement associated with using the Internet to a "high" that video game addicts receive when they play games.

In contrast, Dr. Young's study found that programs used for information gathering or for maintaining relationships that were not real-time or synchronous (e.g., e-mail) were associated with non-dependent Internet users who were not technology addicts. In other words, it appears that the interactive types of programs and applications might have certain features that make them very appealing and prone to addictive behavior. This is a critical issue and is particularly important since social networking is interactive, as are many websites and online activities. In fact, the computer and the technology environment allow for a number of factors that might encourage addiction. In addition to specific programs or applications, a person might become addicted to the act of typing, the type of communication that occurs on the computer or device, the avoidance of face-to-face communication, the kind of information that can be accessed online, or game playing. The fact that so much information and so many activities are available online might intensify the addictive qualities of being on the Internet.

A more complex picture of how the technology itself may spark addictive behaviors involves the rather limited costs and potentially major psychological benefits of our Internet or technology experiences. For example, for minimal time and cost, the Internet in general and social networks in particular allow us to correspond with others who share our interests, meet people we would never otherwise meet, download entertaining software such as games, and keep in touch with friends. Psychologically, we benefit: We gain a feeling of status and trendiness, we are taken seriously and listened to, we can manipulate our online profile to suit our needs and we are allowed to go on and on about interests that our physical family and friends might find very boring.

Addicted to Fun

And we should not forget the fact that programs and applications are designed by humans and companies to be interesting and fun. One of the most important factors that influences our desire and willingness to use technology is the interactivity of the program behind the technology. Psychological rewards, such as those earned while playing video games, also are important and built into the programs by the software designers. Some researchers have likened the sense of excitement associated with using the Internet to a "high" that video game addicts receive when they play games or that gambling addicts receive when they place a bet. With respect to cell phone use, it has been suggested that overuse of the phone (specifically, sending and receiving text messages) results from a need to receive approval from one's friends.

Another possibility is that Internet and technology addiction are part of a larger pattern of technology obsession that goes all the way back to the introduction of radio in the 1930s. With radio, people began getting information and engaging in quasi-social activities through technology-mediated sources. Families gathered around the radio receiver after dinner to listen to the latest shows and to hear up-to-date news. Television continued the trend and the Internet is the latest installment, with smartphones as the ultimate personal resource that allows 24/7 access wherever and whenever.

7

Can Facebook Help Overcome Shyness?

Michael S. Rosenwald

Michael S. Rosenwald is a reporter on The Washington Post's *local enterprise team. He writes about the intersection of technology, business, and culture.*

Facebook can be a boon to shy people who are uncomfortable engaging in conversations in person. The social network can reduce fears about physical appearance or physical reactions and can also provide topics for conversation. Shy people who use the network are sometimes able to more easily talk offline to people they communicate with online. Despite its benefits, though, many shy people who use Facebook still report feeling lonely. Some researchers worry that Facebook may increase shy people's anxieties in some cases, and they warn that more study of Facebook and shyness is needed.

Josh Chiles is shy. In a gathering of unfamiliar people, he often waits for someone, anyone, to ask him a question or make small talk.

At a party, bar or restaurant, "I just sit there, hoping someone will talk to me," he said. "I wait."

Mr. Personality

But on Facebook, the 32-year-old Woodbridge resident is Mr. Personality. He constantly refreshes his status, comments on others' updates, posts pictures, makes jokes and registers his

Michael S. Rosenwald, "Can Facebook Help Overcome Shyness?" *Washington Post*, February 12, 2011. © 2011 Washington Post Company. All rights reserved. Used by permission and protected by the Copyright Laws of the United States. The printing, copying, redistribution, or retransmission of this Content without express written permission is prohibited.

likes. More important, when he sees his digital connections in person, he said, his shyness often disappears.

"There is no doubt that Facebook has improved my life in building relationships with other people," Chiles said.

Chiles is, in many ways, the face of a counterintuitive new stream of research examining whether social networks, particularly Facebook, are for shy people what water is for the thirsty. The studies, with titles such as "The Influence of Shyness on the Use of Facebook" and "Shyness and Online Social Networking Services," grapple with an important question: Can the Age of Oversharing bring the shy and lonely out of their cocoons?

The findings, so far, are tantalizing. Recent studies have shown that shy people are spending more time on Facebook than more socially confident people do, and that the shy report higher satisfaction with the service than do others. Shy people even say they develop closer friendships via the network than the non-shy say they do. One study, published in the journal *CyberPsychology, Behavior and Social Networking*, showed that the Internet and social networks helped lonely children fill "critical needs of social interactions, self-disclosure, and identity exploration."

Though some experts consider Facebook just a crutch for shy people to avoid human contact, many therapists are embracing the technology as a tool that can open social avenues for shy clients. "What we are seeing is that for a lot of shy or socially anxious people, Facebook seems to be getting the ball rolling," said Jonathan Dalton, a therapist at the Behavior Therapy Center of Greater Washington who counsels such people. "Facebook can be used more as a bridge, so to speak."

Even in the slow-connection days of dial-up Internet, the shy and lonely gravitated toward online communication. Hiding behind screen names, they communicated in chat rooms with other screen names, typing back and forth for hours. Early iterations of AOL boasted thousands of chat rooms, and use at night, after the shy and lonely came home from work, spiked. Dalton said he had clients who would tell him their best friend was someone in some distant place, someone they had never met.

> *Social networks such as Facebook make [personal] information available in non-threatening ways, allowing shy people to learn and share without fear of being judged.*

Facebook as a Bridge

Facebook, with its 600 million members, is different. Built by a known shy person—Mark Zuckerberg, who sometimes sweats profusely in TV interviews—the site encourages people to broadcast intimate details of their lives: where they are from, hobbies, favorite TV shows, relationship status, pictures of family, favorite books, jokes, views on religion and politics.

These details are the fabric of everyday conversations and the kindling for relationships. But for shy people, divulging or learning such intimate information is stress-inducing. Some might not try at all, while others might try but blush or sweat, then pull back.

"Shy people have difficulty finding topics to talk about," Dalton said. "Facebook gives you a starting point."

Social networks such as Facebook make such information available in non-threatening ways, allowing shy people to learn and share without fear of being judged on looks or whether they sweat or blush while they talk. In a study published in the *Journal of Social and Personal Relationships*, Levi Baker of the University of Tennessee noted: "Given that learning about others and disclosing personal information often leads to greater intimacy, using social networking services that allow personal information exchanges may facilitate relational development."

"If you avoid people, you isolate, and if you isolate, you are lonely," said Mary Alvord, a Montgomery County psychologist with an interest in social networking. "I am all for anything that can help promote interaction, to start the process."

That was the attraction to Facebook for Ian Luria, a 27-year-old student in Arlington. He had gotten to the point of avoiding most interactions. "My shyness really prevents me from approaching people," he said.

He feels less inhibited on Facebook, where he has more than 230 friends and posts almost every day—funny videos, interesting news stories.

He even used the site to ask out a girl. She said no. Still, he asked, and that was progress.

"I think Facebook has really enhanced my life," Luria said. "It allows me to connect with people I wouldn't connect with otherwise."

Other shy Facebook users and some therapists are not as convinced of the site's benefits, pointing to the downside of relying too much on social networks.

A 33-year-old woman who works in social services in the District—she asked that her name not be published for fear of being embarrassed—said Facebook has made it easier to have conversations around the office with people whose pages she has studied on the network.

Facebook may be better at easing shy people's discomfort with people they know than making them at ease with people generally.

"You can see what they like, and that helps you approach them," she said. "It facilitates a conversation."

But although she's up to 180 friends on Facebook, "I still feel lonely," she said. "I don't feel like I have 180 friends. It's not like I have 180 friends that I can go hang out with. I don't think I have this great social life because I have 180 friends."

Loneliness Remains

Indeed, Baker's study found that even though Facebook deepened relationships, many shy users still reported feeling lonely. Experts suggest that this could be because some shy people use Facebook as a crutch, feeling more comfortable with digital friends than personal ones.

Facebook may be better at easing shy people's discomfort with people they know than making them at ease with people generally.

"Someone who uses Facebook might be less anxious with that person face-to-face, but they may not be learning to feel less anxious when meeting other people at a party or church or an athletic game," said Larry Cohen, a District social worker who counsels shy and socially anxious people. "In fact, anxiety might increase in those cases" because the people don't have the information they glean from Facebook to fall back on.

Cohen said he has seen anxiety increase among some clients who use Facebook because they focus too much on how many friends they have, or worry that others aren't posting enough items on their walls, or fret about what to write in their status updates, just as they agonize over what to say in person.

Cohen suggests to clients that beyond using Facebook, they should sign up for services such as Meetup.com, which arranges in-person meetings for strangers with common interests. In the District, there is even a Meetup group for the shy or socially anxious.

"Overall, I think Facebook is a mixed bag," Cohen said. "The benefits are more obvious, apparent and immediate. But the downsides, at least at first, tend to be less obvious and deeper in the long run. We are really just beginning to understand all of this."

8

Selfies Are Good for Girls

Rachel Simmons

Rachel Simmons is an educator and coach and the author of Odd Girl Out: The Hidden Culture of Aggression in Girls *and* The Curse of the Good Girl: Raising Authentic Girls with Courage and Confidence.

Girls in American culture are discouraged from putting themselves forward or from touting their accomplishments. Sharing "selfies" (self-portraits) on social media gives girls a chance to promote themselves and to take control of their own image. Many argue that selfies are a sign of desperation or that girls are too obsessed with physical appearance. This assumes that girls have no control over their own lives and ignores the extent to which the act of taking selfies pushes back against sexist social standards.

An elementary school principal I once worked with said that if you ask a group of first grade girls who the best runner in the class is, they all point to themselves: *I'm the best runner*, they'll say. Ask a group of sixth grade girls, she went on, and they'll point to the best runner.

Language of the Humble

Ask a group of ninth grade girls, I thought to myself, and when they point out the fast girl, she'll flinch and demur, saying, "No, I'm awful!" Pride, after all, is a cardinal sin in girls'

Rachel Simmons, "Selfies Are Good for Girls," *Slate*, November 20, 2013. © 2013 The Slate Group. All rights reserved. Used by permission and protected by the Copyright Laws of the United States. The printing, copying, redistribution, or retransmission of this Content without express written permission is prohibited.

social culture. It's a lesson they learn early and with ugly consequences. Act too confident and you'll be isolated, called "conceited," a "bitch," a girl who "thinks she's all that," who's "full of herself."

Girls adapt by learning the language of the humble. They raise their hands tentatively at the elbow, beginning classroom comments with apologies ("I'm not sure if this is right, but . . ."). They turn strong opinions into questions with "upspeak." As Amy Schumer lampooned in her viral sketch, young women deflect compliments with frenetic intensity—or, as I've found in my own research, perform an inverse maneuver, earning a compliment by putting themselves down ("I look so awful today." "No you don't, you look amaze!").

When I recently suggested to my Facebook community that selfies might occasionally be a good thing for girls, I was swiftly checked by a chorus of horrified grown-ups.

Enter the selfie, which Oxford Dictionaries just picked as its word of the year [for 2013]. As the Pew Center for Internet Research reported earlier this year, 91 percent of teens have posted one. Last week, the first selfie app went live: Shots of Me, backed by Justin Bieber, is a camera app that opens with the lens already facing its user. These days, the selfie and its main outlet, Instagram, generally come in for much adult loathing. But consider this: The selfie is a tiny pulse of girl pride—a shout-out to the self. Earlier this week, the first three women to complete Marine infantry combat training, along with a fourth who completed most of the hurdles but was injured before her final physical fitness test, posted a jubilant selfie. (Nancy Pelosi tweeted it as "selfie of the year.") If you write off the endless stream of posts as image-conscious narcissism, you'll miss the chance to watch girls practice promoting themselves—a skill that boys are otherwise given more permission to develop, and which serves them later on when they negotiate for raises and promotions.

Casual Self-Promotion

When I posted my first selfie a few months ago after getting a haircut I loved, my thumb hovered, ambivalent, over the post button. I felt a wave of discomfort. How obnoxious, I thought to (and of) myself—are people going to think that I think I look good? And that I want others to know it? That this kind of casual self-promotion comes so easily to girls points to a yawning—and promising—generational divide. Maybe we adult women, of the *Lean In* generation, have something to learn here.

The selfie suggests something in picture form—*I think I look [beautiful] [happy] [funny] [sexy]. Do you?*—that a girl could never get away with saying. It puts the gaze of the camera squarely in a girl's hands, and along with it, the power to influence the photo's interpretation. As psychiatrist Josie Howard recently told Refinery29's Kristin Booker, selfies "may reset the industry standard of beauty to something more realistic." On #selfiesunday, an often giddy end-of-weekend selfiefest, the middle school girls on my feed run the gamut from serious to silly. Some girls are working it, sure, but others have their tongues half out as if to say, I know I look stupid. But I choose to, and I'm beating you to the judgment punch.

When I recently suggested to my Facebook community that selfies might occasionally be a good thing for girls, I was swiftly checked by a chorus of horrified grown-ups. Selfies are a form of "approval seeking," said one. They feel "so desperate," tsked another. Many professionals echo their alarm. Selfies are a sign of low self-esteem, opined a psychologist to *Teen Vogue*. Competitive, said Jess Weiner, Dove's global ambassador for self-esteem.

But of course. Pity the teenage girl. As with sex and hooking up, we assume there is only one motivation and it's a bad one. Girls are perennial victims and the culture always perpetuates this. All girls hook up because they know they'll have to settle to get the intimacy they so desperately crave, even on someone else's terms—not because they might just be drunk and want to make out with someone. All girls sext because they're clueless and stupid—not because some have figured out how to leverage the tools of social media to play at sex without having it. And all girls post selfies because they're desperate for others to fill the beauty-affirmation void left by a ruthless media. Wash, rinse, and repeat.

Not Victims

I've been an educator for the last 15 years. I do worry that for every girl who posts a selfie with pride, others use it to cobble together the validation they cannot give themselves. I worry also about the girls who spend hours editing out their blemishes and adding filters. A 16-year-old from Texas told me that she longs for the days of their grandmothers' brave, set-in-stone Polaroids. And there is plenty that's troubling about girls' tendency to use Instagram to celebrate their physical appearance over their accomplishments. A survey by the Girl Scouts in 2010 found that girls downplayed their intelligence, kindness, and efforts to be a positive influence online in favor of presenting an image that is fun, funny, and social.

But I worry more about a world of parents and educators that are overly invested in seeing all social media as problematic, and positioning girls as passive targets instead of agents of their own lives. Every girl is different, and context matters. The selfie flaunts the restrictions of "good girl" culture like a badass teenager sitting in the back of the classroom, refusing to apologize for what she says. I, for one, want to sit next to her in detention.

9

OMG: Social Media May Wreck Your Kid's Writing

Ruth Campbell

Ruth Campbell covers K-12 and higher education for the Southeast Missourian.

Increasingly, even very young students, such as those in kindergarten and first grade, are familiar with technology and the use of keyboards. Students are more and more likely to do the bulk of their writing on social media or via texting. They become used to leaving out punctuation and using abbreviations. Because of this, they can have trouble switching to more formal English in order to write papers or reports or other assignments. However, familiarity with technology can also be an advantage, since many jobs now require computer and social networking skills.

Convertible laptop computers are being loaded with software Friday for Central High School students to begin using in January [2014]. Teachers say the usage of computers and social media on smartphones has caused students' writing skills to wither.

The prevalence of Facebook, Twitter and texting has all but obliterated punctuation, capitalization and apostrophes in schools, threatening the future of formal writing, educators say.

Ruth Campbell, "OMG: Social Media May Wreck Your Kid's Writing," *Southeast Missourian*, November 24, 2013. Copyright © 2013 by Southeast Missourian. All rights reserved. Reproduced by permission.

Immersed in Technology

And it's no wonder. Cape Girardeau public school students, for example, start learning keyboarding in kindergarten to get them used to technology, curriculum coordinator Theresa Hinkebein said. But she noted kindergartners already know how to operate smartphones and have computers at home.

Keyboarding itself doesn't have an effect on grammar and formal writing, but with people relying more on electronic devices, physical handwriting also is disappearing.

Hinkebein said students are taught cursive writing the second semester of second grade, and kindergarten through 12th-grade students are taught when it's inappropriate to use informal language.

"Our teachers really try to help our students understand the difference between formal and informal writing," she said.

But students come to school "already immersed in technology," Hinkebein noted.

Students are more likely to commit certain grammatical errors because they use the conventions of texting, tweeting and Facebooking in their formal academic essays.

Assistant superintendent for academic services Sherry Copeland said though spell-check and grammar software exist, students still need to know how to spell and use correct grammar. Copeland said she has been on job interviews where a prospective employer has asked her to sit down and write something longhand.

Southeast Missouri State University writing instructor Eric Sentell said in an email to the *Southeast Missourian* that since he began teaching six years ago, he's noticed a difference in the quality of students' writing.

"Students are more likely to commit certain grammatical errors because they use the conventions of texting, tweeting and Facebooking in their formal academic essays. Occasionally, I see actual 'text language,' like using the letter 'u' instead of the word 'you,'" Sentell wrote.

Most of the time, it's lack of capitalization, punctuation and apostrophes, Sentell said.

Code Switching

"Everyone speaks and writes differently for different audiences, but some students struggle to switch between the informal codes of texting and social media and the more-formal codes of standard written English and academic or professional writing. After noticing increases in text language and other grammatical errors, I began emphasizing 'code-switching,' or adapting one's writing to one's audience," Sentell wrote.

"I observed a significant reduction in those errors and an increase in the overall quality of my students' writing. But some capitalization, punctuation and apostrophe errors still creep in every now and then."

Central High School principal Mike Cowan, a former English teacher, said texting language has become so commonplace, he even noticed a billboard between Cape Girardeau and Oak Ridge that used "U" instead of "You."

"If we have a disciplinary situation in school, we always invite the student to write a statement about what happened to try and get down to the facts of the situation. They'll write in that kind of informal expression. I see it more all the time. I think it is indeed an academic battle that faculty teachers are fighting . . ." Cowan said.

For a while, Cowan said he fought texting, but he's doing it himself now.

"Often I'll get comments that I've been texting in complete sentences. Now I'm going for declarative sentences. I guess I've even relented to some degree," he said.

The bottom line, though, is over time people lose writing skills.

"I guess you could argue it's not a loss, but it's a displacement, a change. I'm not so sure how far you can change and still continue to communicate accurately," Cowan said.

Becky Atwood, coordinator of the Cape public school's Adult Education and Literacy Program, said her students are excellent at texting, because that's their primary written communication.

Older students—those in their mid- to late 40s—are "totally lost" on that score, she said.

The two largest age groups served by the Adult Education and Literacy program are 19 to 24 and mid-20s to 40s. Atwood said it doesn't serve "all that many" in the 17- to 18-year-old range.

Different Skills

Atwood said economic and education background affect electronic literacy, as well. "If you were raised . . . middle class or above, you're probably technosavvy," she said. "People in some of the lower income brackets, not so much," because they haven't had access to technology.

"It has affected students' ability to write and write coherently. They have to relearn what they might have already known, or learn new skills that they never mastered, because again, they're used to writing informally and now we're asking them to write with a much more formal . . . purpose, defending their reasoning, and that's not what they're doing when they're communicating, oftentimes, between friends," Atwood said.

Older students, meanwhile, struggle with the basic computer skills that are needed even at lower-paying jobs.

Also, a lot of the assessment tests students take in high school or adult education programs are computer-based.

"They have to have the ability to keyboard and communicate their thoughts in that manner," Atwood said. "The use of pencil and paper is going away."

Over the next year, Atwood said, her program will launch a transitions course in which adult education and literacy staff will work with students on the next steps to take after earning a high school equivalency diploma.

"Because that or a high school diploma will not be enough to earn a living," she said.

Half of teachers say digital tools make it easier to teach writing, 18 percent say those tools make it more difficult.

Adult Education has a resource called Missouri Connections, an online program that allows students to access interest surveys, do research on employment, put together resumes and get information on interviewing.

Missouri Connections also has a section on postsecondary education. "We'll help our students use those resources," Atwood said.

If employment is what students want as their next step, she said, the program will help them, and if further education is the goal, support also is available.

An online survey by the Pew Research Center's Internet & American Life Project, in collaboration with the College Board and the National Writing Project in 2012, conducted among 2,462 middle- and high-school teachers showed while half of teachers say digital tools make it easier to teach writing, 18 percent say those tools make it more difficult.

Socialmediatoday.com notes Twitter has made people more concise, as has blogging.

Meanwhile, teachers in the Pew study "expressed concerns about the 'creep' of informal grammar and style into 'formal' writing, as well as students' impatience with the writing process and their difficulty navigating the complex issues of plagiarism, citation and fair use."

- 68 percent of teachers polled by Pew say digital tools make students more likely to take shortcuts and not put effort into their writing.

- 46 percent said these tools make students more likely to "write too fast and be careless."

10

Social Media Helps Students Write Better

Andrew Simmons

Andrew Simmons is a writer, teacher, and musician. He has written for The New York Times, Slate, *and* The Believer.

Many people argue that the slang encouraged by social media has a bad effect on student writing. However, social media can help students, especially male high school students, reveal emotions and discuss topics that make their writing more powerful and honest. Male students are usually encouraged to be silent, contained, and not reveal emotions. On Facebook, however, students routinely discuss personal issues and emotions and receive praise for doing so. This greater freedom to express themselves improves their writing at school.

*T*he Internet has ruined high-school writing. Write the line on the board five hundred times like [cartoon character] Bart Simpson. Remember and internalize it. Intone it in an Andy Rooney-esque grumble.

I've heard the line repeated by dozens of educators and laypeople. I've even said it myself.

Thankfully it is untrue.

Emoticons vs. Emotional Honesty

As a high-school English teacher, I read well over a thousand student essays a year. I can report that complete sentences are an increasingly endangered species. I wearily review the point

Andrew Simmons, "Facebook Has Transformed My Students' Writing—For the Better," *Atlantic*, November 18, 2013. © 2013 The Atlantic Media Co, as first published in The Atlantic Magazine. All rights reserved. Distributed by Tribune Content Agency, LLC. Reproduced by permission.

of paragraphs every semester. This year I tried and failed to spark a senior class protest against "blobs"—my pejorative term for essays lacking paragraphs. When I see a winky face in the body of a personal essay—and believe me, it has happened enough to warrant a routine response—I use a red pen to draw next to it a larger face with narrow, angry eyes and gaping jaws poised to chomp the offending emoticon to pieces Pac-Man-style. My students analyze good writing and discuss the effect of word choice and elegant syntax on an audience's reading experience. The uphill battle is worth fighting, but I'm always aware that something more foreboding than chronic senioritis lines up in opposition.

However, while Facebook and Twitter have eroded writing conventions among my students, they have not killed the most important ingredients in personal writing: self-reflection and emotional honesty. For younger high school boys particularly, social networking has actually improved writing—not the product or the process, but the sensitivity and inward focus required to even begin to produce a draft that will eventually be worth editing.

High school is cruel to all genders, an equal-opportunity destroyer of spirit and self-esteem. I'm focusing on boys because I've seen the phenomenon play out more intensely with them. Also, I was a boy once, and so I understand them better than I understand girls.

The emotional distance fostered by Facebook and other sites can encourage a healthier candor.

When I was beginning high school in 1994 boys knew not to reveal weakness and insecurity. Girls didn't seem to like guys who vocalized vulnerability. Athletes usually projected stereotypically masculine traits: along with imposing physical size, aggressive, even belligerent confidence, an easy stance, gait, and casual presence, the signs of being comfortable in their own skins. Even the scrawniest punk guitarists wore hoodies like armor and possessed a prickly toughness seasoned by the experience of having been bullied in middle school. The climate demanded stoicism, cool detachment as the default attitude for boys trying not to lose social standing. Young male attitudes were, as they still are, shaped by music and other forms of pop culture. Mainstream mid-90s rappers had cold-blooded personas. Even [rock singer for Nirvana] Kurt Cobain mumbled through interviews, only opening up in cathartic song, where the rawest admissions could be obtuse and readily cloaked in distortion. Everyone agonized over problems—height, acne, academic ability, body size, a lack of attention from girls, parents splitting up, sick grandparents, needy siblings, general alienation—but no one wanted to talk about them much. At age 14, I was small, smart, and artistic. I wrote well, but the prospect of writing anything that would permit even a teacher to know what I really thought terrified me. Spilling my guts in a writers' workshop with my classmates would have been social suicide.

Social networking has dramatically altered how highschool boys deal with their emotions.

Watching Facebook

I have a Facebook page dedicated solely to my position as an educator. I don't send friend requests to students but current and former students can send them to me and I always accept. I don't post much, but I keep up with some students and share literature-related links when I delude myself into thinking they'll be of interest. Current students often send me requests without thinking of the possible consequences of being Facebook friends with a teacher. I have made it a policy to avoid bringing a student's posts into a conference with a parent or counselor unless required to do so by law. A few times a week though, I log on and observe what students post.

My observations have reaffirmed the widely held notion that the Internet is no refuge from the pains of adolescence. It's a really bad neighborhood. On Facebook and Twitter, students humiliate, jeer, and shame one another. They engage in antisocial, even criminal behavior—leaving belligerently racist comments on links, harassing classmates with derogatory posts.

At the same time, the emotional distance fostered by Facebook and other sites can encourage a healthier candor, too. On Facebook, even popular students post statuses in which they express insecurities. I see a dozen every time I log on. A kid frets that his longtime girlfriend is straying and wishes he hadn't upset her. Another admits to being lonely (with weepy emoticons added for effect). Another asks friends to pray for his sick little sister. Another worries the girl he gave his number to isn't interested because she hasn't called in the 17 minutes that have passed since the fateful transaction. Another disparages his own intellect. "I'm so stupid, dad told me to drop out," he writes. Another wonders why his parents are always angry, and why their anger is so often directed at him. "Brother coming home today," another posts. "Gonna see how it goes."

Individually these may seem like small-scale admissions. But the broader trend I have witnessed in the past few years stands in sharp contrast to the vigilance with which my generation guarded our fears both trivial and deep. In this sense, social networking has dramatically altered how high-school boys deal with their emotions.

Instead of being mocked for revealing too much, students who share in this way win likes and supportive comments from male friends. Perhaps part of it is the fact that girls appear to appreciate the emotional candor and publicly validate it with likes and comments, giving boys the initiative to do the same. In high-school halls, guards stay up, but online, male emotional transparency is not only permitted but also celebrated. Surely, the current crop of "sensitive" rappers has also encouraged this—especially standard-bearer Kanye West, who treats albums like therapy sessions and doesn't mind welling up on national television. In addition to their insecurities, boys share affectionate admissions of platonic love to one another that they wouldn't feel as comfortable sharing in person. They post "I admit" and "To be honest" notes on one another's pages in which they celebrate fraternal bonds.

Just as social networking frees users from public decorum ... it allows my students to safely, if temporarily, construct kinder, gentler versions of themselves as well.

"You my bro cause you always have time to talk."

"Even when there no one else you got me."

However trite, these public expressions may be the seeds of richer revelations.

Writing as Healing

Because it happens on the Internet, the candor is a simulation of how a more evolved young male culture might operate. Despite the Drake pics captioned with the rapper's soft-headed couplets, the fight videos, and the countless time-wasting surveys and games that pollute the average high-school student's feed, I see the online social universe my students traverse as an improvement over my high-school terrain. Many of my students grow up in households in which machismo reigns supreme. They've never been allowed to cry. Their mothers and sisters cook and wash the dishes and clean. They've been encouraged to see themselves as dominant, powerful, swaggering, sullen men, not sensitive and reflective men, powerfully kind, confidently open. Fostering those traits is a woman's responsibility, like housework. In this sense, Facebook is a genuine outlet for the young men I teach. Just as social networking frees users from public decorum and encourages the birthing of troll alter egos, it allows my students to safely, if temporarily, construct kinder, gentler versions of themselves as well.

The great news is that this has a positive effect on teaching and learning. My students in 2013 are more comfortable writing about personal issues than were my classmates in the mid-late '90s. When I assign narrative essays, students discuss sexual abuse, poverty, imprisoned family members, alcoholic parents, gang violence, the struggle to learn English in America—topics they may need to address, not merely subjects they believe might entertain or interest a reader.

After all, we write for an audience and we write for ourselves too. I see students recognizing the value of tackling these topics with honesty. I notice that they are relieved when they do so. Sometimes students address the same topic in several essays over the course of the year, updating me, their confidante, on the status of a specific situation. When they share these essays with the rest of the class, they turn the two-way conversation (their writing, my feedback) into a network. Writing isn't just about the spilling of guts, obviously, but the transparency encouraged by social networking has laid the foundation for this freedom. When this freedom results in powerful, honest writing, it can in turn result in true healing for kids—not just the momentary reassurance a well-received status update may provide.

Organizations to Contact

The editors have compiled the following list of organizations concerned with the issues debated in this book. The descriptions are derived from materials provided by the organizations. All have publications or information available for interested readers. The list was compiled on the date of publication of the present volume; the information here may change. Be aware that many organizations take several weeks or longer to respond to inquiries, so allow as much time as possible.

American Library Association (ALA)
50 E. Huron, Chicago, IL   60611
(800) 545-2433
website: www.ala.org

The American Library Association (ALA) is the oldest and largest library association in the world, with more than sixty-five thousand members. Its mission is to promote the highest quality library and information services and public access to information. ALA offers professional services and publications to members and nonmembers. The association supports the use of social networking sites in libraries and classrooms as a part of economic, civic, and cultural life.

Amnesty International
5 Penn Plaza, 14th Floor, New York, NY   10001
(212) 807-8400 • fax: (212) 463-9193
e-mail: aimember@aiusa.org
website: www.amnestyusa.org

Amnesty International is a worldwide movement of people who campaign for internationally recognized human rights. Its vision is of a world in which every person enjoys all of the human rights enshrined in the Universal Declaration of Human Rights and other international human rights standards. Each year it publishes a report on its work and its concerns throughout the world. Its website includes numerous posts that discuss social networking in the context of human rights, such as "Don't Fear the Tweets, Fear the Tweeters" and "Tear Gas Fired and Websites Blocked as Belarus Protesters Are Targeted."

Association of Internet Marketing & Sales (AIMS)
e-mail: admin@aimscanada.com
website: www.aimscanada.com

The Association of Internet Marketing & Sales (AIMS) is a Canadian association for businesspeople looking to use the Internet to reach customers and expand. Its members include interactive marketers, salespeople, executives, developers, designers, consultants, business owners, and many others. AIMS delivers education, networking, and discussion through events and online community building initiatives. Its website includes news, a blog, and information about AIMS events.

Berkman Center for Internet & Society
23 Everett St., 2nd Floor, Cambridge, MA 02138
(617) 495-7547 • fax: (617) 495-7641
e-mail: cyber@law.harvard.edu
website: http://cyber.law.harvard.edu

The Berkman Center for Internet & Society conducts research on legal, technical, and social developments in cyberspace and assesses the need or lack thereof for laws and sanctions. It publishes a monthly newsletter, *The Filter*, blog posts, and articles based on the Center's research efforts, many of which are available on its website, including the final report of the Internet Safety Technical Task Force, *Enhancing Child Safety & Online Technologies*, and "Insights on Cyberbullying: An Interview with a Digital Native," a news report from Berkman's Digital Natives Reporters in the Field.

Center for Democracy & Technology (CDT)
1634 I St. NW, #1100, Washington, DC 20006
(202) 637-9800 • fax: (202) 637-0968
website: www.cdt.org

The mission of the Center for Democracy & Technology (CDT) is to develop public policy solutions that advance constitutional civil liberties and democratic values in new computer and communications media. Pursuing its mission through policy research, public education, and coalition building, the Center works to increase citizens' privacy and the public's control over the use of personal information held by government and other institutions. Its publications include issue briefs, policy papers, and CDT Policy Posts.

Electronic Frontier Foundation (EFF)
454 Shotwell St., San Francisco, CA   94110-1914
(415) 436-9333 • fax: (415) 436-9993
e-mail: information@eff.org
website: www.eff.org

The Electronic Frontier Foundation (EFF) is an organization of students and other individuals that aims to promote a better understanding of telecommunications issues. It fosters awareness of civil liberties issues arising from advancements in computer-based communications media and supports litigation to preserve, protect, and extend First Amendment rights in computing and telecommunications technologies. EFF's publications include the electronic newsletter *EFFector Online* and online bulletins and publications, including "Did Twitter, Facebook Really Build a Revolution?" and "Early Lessons from the Tunisian Revolution."

Federal Trade Commission (FTC)
600 Pennsylvania Ave. NW, Washington, DC   20580
(877) 382-4357
website: www.ftc.gov

The Federal Trade Commission (FTC) is the federal agency that regulates commerce, economic activity, consumer protection, and competition. Its website offers information on online privacy and security issues such as identity theft, Internet fraud, and protecting kids online and on social networks. The

FTC maintains OnGuardOnline.gov, which provides information about Internet scams, viruses, and other Internet security and privacy issues.

Global Internet Freedom Consortium
e-mail: contact@internetfreedom.org
website: www.internetfreedom.org

The Global Internet Freedom Consortium is a consortium of organizations that develop and deploy anticensorship technologies for use by Internet users in countries whose governments restrict Internet-based information access. It has especially focused on Internet freedom in China. Its website includes information about the organization's activities, white papers, and research reports, such as "Battle for Freedom in Chinese Cyberspace" and "Report on Google.cn's Self Censorship."

Internet Services Providers' Association, United Kingdom (ISPA UK)
1 Castle Lane, London   SW1E 6DR
020 3397 3304 • fax: 0871 594 0298
e-mail: admin@ispa.org.uk
website: www.ispa.org.uk

The Internet Services Providers' Association, United Kingdom (ISPA UK) is the United Kingdom's trade association for Internet service providers. Its mission is to provide essential support for Internet services and promote collaboration between its members and the wider Internet community. It advocates before government bodies on behalf of the Internet industry and users. ISPA publishes *Political Monitor*, a weekly newsletter for members on political issues affecting the Internet industry. Its website also includes press releases and information about events and policies.

Internet Society (ISOC)
1775 Wiehle Ave., Suite 102, Reston, VA   20190-5108
(703) 326-2120 • fax: (703) 326-9881

e-mail: isoc@isoc.org
website: www.isoc.org

A group of technologists, developers, educators, researchers, government representatives, and businesspeople, the Internet Society (ISOC) supports the development and dissemination of standards for the Internet and works to ensure global cooperation and coordination for the Internet and related Internetworking technologies and applications. It publishes the *IETF Journal*, a newsletter, and annual reports.

Bibliography

Books

Mark Bauerlein	*The Digital Divide: Arguments For and Against Facebook, Google, Texting, and the Age of Social Networking.* New York: Penguin Group, 2011.
Danah Boyd	*It's Complicated: The Social Lives of Networked Teens.* New Haven, CT: Yale University Press, 2014.
Nicholas Carr	*The Shallows: What the Internet Is Doing to Our Brains.* New York: W.W. Norton, 2011.
Manuel Catells	*Networks of Outrage and Hope: Social Movements in the Internet Age.* Malden, MA: Polity Press, 2012.
Jose van Dijck	*The Culture of Connectivity: A Critical History of Social Media.* New York: Oxford University Press, 2013.
Shawn Marie Edgington	*The Parent's Guide to Texting, Facebook, and Social Media: Understanding the Benefits and Dangers of Parenting in a Digital World.* Dallas, TX: Brown Books, 2011.
Elizabeth Kandel Englander	*Bullying and Cyberbullying: What Every Educator Needs to Know.* Cambridge, MA: Harvard Education Press, 2013.

Christian Fuchs   *Social Media: A Critical Introduction.* Thousand Oaks, CA: Sage Publications, 2013.

Joe Grimm, ed.   *The New Bullying—How Social Media, Social Exclusion Laws and Suicide Have Changed Our Definition of Bullying, and What to Do About It.* Canton, MI: David Crumm Media, 2012.

Mizuko Ito et al.   *Living and Learning with New Media: Summary of Findings from the Digital Youth Project.* Cambridge, MA: MIT Press, 2009.

Robert W. McChesney   *Digital Disconnect: How Capitalism Is Turning the Internet Against Democracy.* New York: The New Press, 2013.

Tom Standard   *Writing on the Wall: Social Media—The First 2,000 Years.* New York: Bloomsbury, 2013.

Clive Thompson   *Smarter than You Think: How Technology Is Changing Our Minds for the Better.* New York: Penguin Books, 2013.

Daniel Trottier   *Social Media as Surveillance.* Burlington, VT: Ashgate Publishing, 2012.

Sherry Turkle   *Alone Together: Why We Expect More from Technology and Less from Each Other.* Philadelphia: Basic Books, 2011.

Periodicals and Internet Sources

Sarah Boesveld	"'Overblown and Sensationalized': Author Says Bullying Issue Is More Nuanced than Black and White," *National Post*, February 23, 2013. http://news.nationalpost.com.
Art Caplan	"Is Your Doctor Spying on Your Tweets? Social Media Raises Medical Privacy Questions," NBC News, October 21, 2013. www.nbcnews.com.
Daniel Etcovitch	"Social Media Doesn't Hurt My Offline Social Abilities, It Helps Them," *Huffington Post*, November 18, 2013. www.huffingtonpost.com.
Sam Fiorella	"Cyber-Bullying, Social Media, and Parental Responsibility," *Huffington Post*, October 18, 2013. www.huffingtonpost.com.
Michelle Goldberg	"In Defense of Jonathan Franzen," *Daily Beast*, September 26, 2013. www.thedailybeast.com.
Lesley Kinzel	"Leave Selfies Alone," *xojane*, November 22, 2013. www.xojane.com.
Larry Magid	"Common Sense Media Report Shines Positive Light on Kids and Social Media," *Huffington Post*, June 26, 2012. www.huffingtonpost.com.

Irene Maher   "Social Media Can Become an
                     Addiction, but You Can Break Free,"
                     Tampa Bay Times, July 25, 2013.

Claire Murphy   "The Dangers of Being Always On,"
                     PR Week, November 28, 2013.
                     www.prweek.com.

Nature World   "Social Networking Sites Promoting
News   Eating Disorders," October 5, 2013.
                     www.natureworldnews.com.

John Naughton   "Twitter and the Transformation of
                     Democracy," *Guardian*, September 14,
                     2013.

Walter Pacheco   "Professor Says Teens' Social-Media
                     Lingo Hurts Writing Skills," *Orlando
                     Sentinel*, July 18, 2012.

Phys.org   "Researchers Explore the Impact of
                     Social Networking on Shyness," July
                     5, 2010. http://phys.org.

Ryan Singel   "Google Tweaks Buzz After
                     Overblown Privacy Backlash," *Wired*,
                     February 17, 2010. www.wired.com.

Lauren Slavin   "The Evolution of Selfie Culture:
                     Self-Expression, Narcissism, or
                     Objectification?," *feminspire*, 2013.
                     http://feminspire.com.

Adam Tanner   "Users More Savvy About Social
                     Media Privacy than Thought, Poll
                     Finds," *Forbes*, November 13, 2013.

Gunnes Tavmen   "The Pathology of Expecting Social Network Websites to Wave the 'Democracy Flag,'" OpenDemocracy, October 21, 2013. www.opendemocracy.net.

Clive Thompson   "Teenagers and Social Networking—It Might Actually Be Good for Them," *Guardian*, October 4, 2013.

David Trifunov   "Texting, Social Media Might Be Creating Better Student Writers, Study Says," GlobalPost, July 17, 2013. www.globalpost.com.

Katy Waldman   "Jonathan Franzen's Lonely War on the Internet Continues," *Slate*, October 4, 2013. www.slate.com.

ALLEN PARK PUBLIC LIBRARY #4

Index

J

K

L

M

N

O

P

DISCARD